P9-DCB-895

# BERLITZ®

# CYPRUS

Please Read
**Do Not Destroy**

- A ☑ in the text denotes a highly recommended sight
- A complete A–Z of practical information starts on p. 107
- Extensive mapping throughout: on cover flaps and in text

Copyright © **1993** by Berlitz Publishing Co Ltd, Berlitz House, Peterley Road, Oxford OX4 2TX, England.

All rights reserved. No part of this book may be reproduced or transmitted in any form or by any means, electronic or mechanical, including photocpying, recording or by any information storage and retrieval system without permission in writing from the publisher.

Berlitz Trademark Reg. US Patent Office and other countries. Marca Registrada.

Printed in Switzerland by Weber SA, Bienne.

2nd edition 1993/4

**Although we make every effort to ensure the accuracy of the information in this guide, changes do occur. If you have any new information, suggestions or corrections to contribute, we would like to hear from you. Please write to Berlitz Publishing at the above address.**

Text: Jack Altman

Photography: Jon Davison

Staff Editor: Jane Middleton

Cartography: 🅕ᴀʟᴋ Falk-Verlag, Hamburg

Thanks to: Georghios Ph. Kyriakides of the Anonymous Beach Hotel, Ayia Napa, Chris Loizou Watersports Ltd, Sandy Beach, Ayia Napa, and Dimitris Georgiou of GDK Rent a Car, Larnaca, for their cooperation in allowing access for some of the photographs to be taken.

*Cover picture*: Monastery of Ayia Napa

# CONTENTS

# Cyprus and the Cypriots

The pleasures of Cyprus derive above all from its apparent simplicity – the straightforward physical charm of the island and the natural warmth of the people. In a sea of troubles at the eastern end of the Mediterranean, Cyprus surmounts its own problems to offer a remarkably reassuring haven of calm.

The coastline has enough rugged cliffs and surf-beaten coves to appeal to the romantic individualist and sufficient well-organized modern seaside beach resorts to keep the family happy, too. In the plains of the interior, villages nestle among olive groves and citrus orchards. Goats and sheep scamper among ruins of ancient Greek temples and Roman markets. Vineyards climb the sunny hillsides and, higher up, cypress trees frame a somnolent abbey or the skeleton of an abandoned fortress. Yes, this is a Mediterranean island.

Yet not just any old Mediterranean island. It has a character that is European by historic links to Greece, but also Levantine through involvement from ancient to modern times with Syria and Turkey, and even a touch of Africa via Egypt to the south. A first hint of this complexity comes as soon as you get into town. Away from the seafront in the port towns of Limassol and Larnaca, but especially in the inland capital of Nicosia, the juxtaposition on the skyline of a mosque's minaret and the dome of an Orthodox church reminds you of the island's tragic division between Greek and Turkish Cypriots.

# A Land of Good Living

Nicosia, capital of Cyprus since the 12th century, rises up out of the Mesaoria plain, baked dry in summer and bedecked with flowers and orchard blossoms in the spring. Mesaoria means 'between the mountains': to the north-east, **5**

*Faded pastel facades in the pretty village of Kato Drys.*

the craggy Kyrenia range runs into the narrow Karpas Peninsula, outstretched finger of the island's pointing-fist silhouette; and to the south-west, the wooded slopes of the Troodos mountains capture enough winter snow to make for good skiing at higher altitudes. De-

pleted since ancient times because the wood has been used for ship building, the Paphos Forest of the western mountains has been restored, thanks to an initiative in 1907 by a young under-secretary at the British Colonial Office named Winston Churchill.

This is healthy country. The old diseases of malaria and tapeworm have been eradicated and the climate is good. Hot dry summers from June to September range between an average low of 21°C (69°F) and average high of 37°C (98°F). Winters from November to March are rainy, with temperatures from 5°C (41°F) to 15°C (59°F). Short sharp changes come with spring in April/May and autumn in October.

Cyprus made its ancient fortune from the copper which gave the island its name and colours its silhouette on the Republic's national flag. Today, Cyprus has struck gold with tourism, but also collects good revenues from exporting clothes, fruit and wine. A highly appreciated legacy of British rule is the network of first-class roads, easily the best in the eastern Mediterranean and a great boon for visitors wanting to explore the island on their own.

# Much More Than Greek

The ancient myth is that Aphrodite, goddess of love, was born here and ever since, it seems, everyone has wanted a piece of her island. Apart from attracting Phoenician and

---

### The Attila Line

The boundary separating northern Turkish-occupied Cyprus from the Greek-Cypriot Republic since 1974 (see p. 26) is rarely seen by most visitors. A wall and barbed wire divide north and south Nicosia, while holidaymakers driving up from Agia Napa in the island's south-east corner may glimpse an observation post for troops of the United Nations and the Turkish Army on the outskirts of the old port town of Famagusta.

It is complicated, but not impossible, for visitors from the south to cross into northern Cyprus (via Nicosia). For the day when the whole island can be visited without difficulty, we describe both regions, but with emphasis on the larger more easily accessible southern portion.

Assyrian pirates, conquerors from Egypt and Persia, and the ever-belligerent Greeks and Turks, Cyprus has been the easy prey of French Crusaders, Venetian and Genoese merchants, and a pawn in the last days of the British Empire. (Novelist Lawrence Durrell's *Bitter Lemons*, on his days in Cyprus as teacher and colonial official, is beautifully written but most reveals just how paternalistic even the best-intentioned British observer could be in the fateful 1950s.)

All these visitors, some more welcome than others, have left their traces, from the Greek basilica and temples of Kourion (near Limassol) to the splendid mosaics of Roman villas at Paphos; Crusaders' castles in the Kyrenia mountains and Gothic churches in Famagusta; Venetian bastions in Nicosia and Byzantine monasteries in the Troodos mountains; Turkish mosques in all the big towns, north and south; and, most recent and cosiest of archaeological relics, the British pillar boxes (repainted yellow) and Belisha

beacons (still orange) at the zebra crossings. Slightly less charming vestiges of imperial might are the British military bases – 'Sovereign Base Areas' – on the south coast and the Turkish counterparts in the north.

Since the historical struggle for union with Greece was relinquished in favour of the island's independence in 1960, Greek Cypriots have come increasingly to recognize their distinctive national identity. Their Orthodox Church is autocephalous, which means that the Archbishop is head of the national church independent of any patriarch outside Cyprus. The Islam of Turkish Cypriots is of the moderate Sunni persuasion.

Considering their turbulent history, one cannot but marvel at the Cypriots' quiet, easy-going nature. They have the sunny disposition you may expect (though don't always find) in the Mediterranean. People in the remotest mountain village can be immensely hospitable. The stranger is no enemy. In the tavernas away

## Geography

Tucked into the north-east corner between Turkish Anatolia and Syria, Cyprus is the third largest island in the Mediterranean, after Sicily and Sardinia. Its land surface of 9,251 sq km (3,572 sq miles) sandwiches the broad Mesaoria Plain between two chains of mountains – the Kyrenia (or Pentadaktylos 'Five Fingers') range in the north-east and the Troodos range in the south-west. Three major rivers – running dry in summer – originate in the Troodos mountains: the Pedieos flowing east to Famagusta Bay, the Karyoti west to Morphou Bay and the Kouris south to Episkopi. The highest peak is Mount Olympus in the Troodos range at 1,951 m (6,401 ft).

## Population

752,000 (171,000 in the Turkish-occupied north: 80,000 are post-1974 settlers from Anatolia and 35,000 Turkish soldiers).

## Capital

Nicosia (220,800, including 41,060 in the Turkish-Cypriot sector).

## Major cities

Limassol (135,000), Larnaca (63,000), Paphos (29,000), Famagusta (21,330), Morphou (11,180), Kyrenia (7,580).

## Government

The Republic of Cyprus was set up in 1960 as a parliamentary democracy with a Greek-Cypriot President and a Turkish-Cypriot Vice-President. The House of Representatives was divided on a ratio of 7 to 3 among Greek Cypriots and Turkish Cypriots, until the latter withdrew their Vice-President in 1963. Covering 37% of the island, the 'Turkish Republic of Northern Cyprus' was proclaimed in 1983 and recognized only by Turkey. It has a president, prime minister and legislative assembly.

## Religion

In the Republic of Cyprus 98% of the population is Eastern Orthodox and 2% Maronite, Armenian, Catholic and Moslem; in Turkish-occupied Northern Cyprus 99% are Sunni Moslem.

from the tourist-oriented watering-holes, you will often find yourself engaged in friendly banter with 'locals' at the neighbouring table.

This widespread cheerfulness is coupled with real dignity that shuns expansive surface gestures. The British like to think that their presence on the island over the past century has been at least partly responsible, and as far as the politeness of the police and the sober honesty of public officials are concerned, they may be right. But the courtesy of the Cypriots in general seems to be a more deeply ingrained quality coming from a heartfelt concern for their fellows.

A more sombre note is struck when the question of the divided island is raised. Greek Cypriot refugees from the north – there were some 170,000 in 1974, with about 30,000 Turkish Cypriots going in the opposite direction – react with more melancholy than anger. Nostalgically, restaurants and shops in Larnaca or Limassol may bear the names of their lost homes in Famagusta, Kyrenia or Bellapais. Under military occupation, Turkish Cypriots speak less easily of the division but make the distinction between those born on the island, decidedly ambivalent, and the peasants brought in from Turkish Anatolia after 1974, who remain tight-lipped.

In addition to the British military community, which is most visible around Limassol and Larnaca Bay, the Republic's foreign residents are mostly Levantine neighbours – Lebanese and Armenian Christians, even a few Arab Moslems.

The island's prosperity and ethnic mix make dining out a pleasant adventure. The copious *mezedes* (hors d'oeuvres) provide a feast in themselves, spiced with the influences of Greek, Turkish and Levantine cooking. The locally brewed beer is excellent and the brandy lusty, but it is the Cypriot wine that stands out, offering the fine amiable distinction that characterizes the people themselves.

# A Brief History

The first records of human presence in Cyprus seem to be those of a group who were 'tourists' rather than permanent residents. Tools and butchered animal bones found in a cave on the south coast are dated at about 8500 BC; the bones are thought to be the remains of pygmy hippopotamus killed and barbecued on the beach by a group of seafarers, who landed briefly on the island.

The earliest traces of permanent settlers are sturdy stone beehive house dwellings at the northern tip of the Karpas peninsula and the inland site of Khirokitia in the south, which date back at least to 7000 BC. Hunters and farmers lived in sizeable communities of up to 2,000. They preferred to use vessels ground from stone rather than moulded in clay.

## The Kindness of Strangers

By 3500 BC, copper was being mined in the Troodos foothills. Cyprus began to prosper as a trading centre, with goods coming in from Asia, Egypt, Crete, the Peloponnese and the Aegean islands in exchange for Cypriot pottery, copperware and a much appreciated crop of

---

**Home from Home**

Salamis, for long the island's principal city, was founded according to legend by Teucer, brother of Ajax, a hero of the Trojan wars, and himself a courageous archer. It was named after the Greek island where Teucer was born, just west of Athens. His father banished him for returning home without the body of his dead brother. Heartbroken, for Teucer had at least struggled valiantly to assure his beloved brother an honourable burial, he sailed east again, to settle in Cyprus.

opium. To please the varied clientèle, Cypriot potters mixed Aegean and Oriental motifs – flowers, lions and sphinxes. The island's crossroads destiny was already emerging.

After 1600 BC, large numbers of fortresses were built around the island, which suggests a period of conflict. Copper was sent to mighty Egypt as protection money and, in exchange, the Pharoah called the king of Cyprus 'brother'.

Upheaval in the Peloponnese caused variously by natural calamities and invasions from the north drove Mycenaean Greeks east across the Mediterranean. Some, said Homer, went to fight the

*T*he magnificent ruin of the Sanctuary of Apollo Hylates at Kourion is nearly 2,000 years old.

Trojan Wars. A few settled in Cyprus. From 1200 BC, they established city-kingdoms at Enkomi, replaced later by Salamis (near modern Famagusta), Kition (now Larnaca), Kourion and Paphos in the south, Soloi and Lapithos in the north. The island acquired the predominantly Greek identity it was never to relinquish. The Greeks brought new skills in architecture, pottery, fine ivory carving and the copper and iron industries. Temples were erected near smelting workshops, presided over by Aphrodite, goddess of fertility, and Hephaestos, the divine blacksmith.

## East–West Tensions

In the 9th century, Kition, left in ruins by an earthquake, was resettled by Phoenicians from Tyre in Syria. Dedicated to Astarte, Oriental counterpart to Aphrodite, their temple was similar in design to Solomon's Phoenician-built temple in Jerusalem. The dynamic coexistence of Greek and Oriental communities on Cyprus was reflected by the tombs at Salamis. After being buried like the Greek heroes of the Trojan Wars, with chariot and sacrifical horses and cattle, the dead were festooned with opulent Oriental treasure.

Just as it was to become in modern times a pawn in the conflicts between Greece and Turkey, so Cyprus was caught up in the ancient power struggles of Persia and Greece. The Persian Empire spread across the eastern Mediterranean in the 6th century, annexing Cyprus along with other Greek islands. In 499, Cyprus joined the Ionian Greek revolt but was crushed the following year by the Persian army after heroic resistance, notably during the prolonged siege of Paphos.

The Persians supported Phoenician expansion into the valuable inland copper belt. King Evagoras of Salamis countered by consolidating Greek power across the island with backing from the Athenians. Artistic styles reflected the king's Hellenistic preferences: decorative Attic pottery, **13**

## Paul Does His Stuff

With Cypriot-born Barnabas, the apostle Paul came from Syria to bring the new word of Christianity to the synagogues of Salamis. They were given short shrift and went off to Paphos where, the New Testament says, 'they found a certain sorcerer, a false prophet, a Jew'. To punish this fellow Elymas for keeping them away from the Roman proconsul, Paul struck him blind. The proconsul, 'when he saw what was done, believed, being astonished at the doctrine of the Lord'.

Classical sculpture in native Cypriot bronze, terracotta, limestone and as well as marble imported by Athenian émigrés in Salamis. Persian motifs showed up in the finely crafted jewellery, and the architecture of massive fortifications for these troubled times was also clearly Persian.

## From Alexander to the Caesars

In 333 BC, Alexander the Great ended Persian supremacy in the eastern Mediterranean and placed Cyprus under Macedonian rule, introducing Macedonian coinage and Greek weights and measures. **14** His generals used the island as a battleground for the succession, destroying Kition, Lapithos, Marion and Kyrenia in the process. By 299 BC, Ptolemy I emerged the victor and the city-kingdoms disappeared as Cyprus became part of the Hellenistic state of Egypt. The Ptolemies ruled for 250 years until the Romans, on a pretext that the island was harbouring pirates threatening their interests, annexed it to their province of Cilicia (southern coast of modern Turkey).

While in Egypt in 48 BC, Julius Caesar made a present of the island to Cleopatra, last illustrious member of the Ptolemy dynasty. After her suicide, Augustus took it back for the Roman Empire. He let his vassal, King Herod of Judaea, farm out the Cypriot copper concession to Jewish entrepreneurs and this led to the only disruption in 300 years of *Pax Romana*. In AD 116, Jewish revolts spread from Egypt and Libya to Cyprus. No Roman troops were kept in what had become a tranquil backwater and the Jews went on a murderous rampage until an army arrived under Libyan general Lucius Quietus and exterminated the whole community.

## The Byzantine Era

Despite the apostle Paul's mission to Cyprus in AD 45, Paphos led the resolutely Hellenistic islanders in the cults of Aphrodite and, with the growth of highly prized vineyards, the wine god Dionysos. Only in the 4th cen-

tury, as Christianity took a hold on the Roman leadership, did churches and monasteries begin to spring up across Cyprus.

In 330, the year that Constantinople became the imperial capital, the Christian Empress Helena is said to have visited the island and founded the great Stavrovouni monastery with a piece of the True Cross as its most cherished relic. Also around this time,

*Water fountain fresco at the monastery of Ayios Minas.*

the church won more friends when a special breed of cats reared at St Nicholas monastery on the Akrotiri peninsula rid the island of a plague of snakes.

Earthquakes levelled Paphos in 332 and Salamis 10 years later. The latter was rebuilt and made the capital under the new name of Constantia.

Priests wielded considerable power over everyday life, defending peasants against grasping tax collectors, but also demanding unquestioning allegiance. In a prolonged power struggle with the Patriarch of Antioch (Syria), in 488 the Archbishop of Cyprus gained undisputed control over the island's spiritual affairs. He won Emperor Zeno over to his cause by presenting him with the original manuscript of Matthew's gospel discovered in the tomb of Barnabas, founder of the Church of Cyprus. The archbishop was henceforth authorized to carry a sceptre rather than pastoral staff and sign his name in imperial purple ink.

## Rise of Islam

With the Byzantine Empire too weak from its 7th-century war against Persia to resist the Moslem advance in Palestine, Syria and Egypt, the Arabs were emboldened to cross over to Cyprus in 649 with a fleet of 1,500 ships. Constantia-Salamis was left in ruins from which it was never to recover and the raid continued across the island until news of an approaching Byzantine fleet prompted retreat.

Four years later, in a move that uncannily foreshadowed events of the 20th century,

### The Worms That Turned

In the 6th century, two monks contributed to the island's wealth by revealing closely guarded secrets of the Chinese silk industry. They combined their mission to spread the gospel with a little industrial espionage, smuggling a few silkworms out of China concealed in their holy rods.

the Arabs staged a second invasion and left a garrison of 12,000 men, encouraging Moslem immigration to establish a foothold. The Byzantine and Moslem Caliphate subsequently agreed by treaty to neutralize Cyprus – no military bases, though ports could be used for refitting the navy – and share tax revenues. Over the next 300 years, offshore battles and Moslem and Byzantine raids did occur, but Moslems and Christians lived side by side in more harmony than their own respective historical accounts may now suggest. Though Moslem villages were concentrated mostly in the east, Paphos remained in Moslem hands and Greek Cypriots moved inland to a new community at Ktima and from Kourion to Episkopi.

Both rulers used Cyprus as a place to park their more troublesome rebels. Typically, emperors who had outlawed icons happily sent their image-worshipping monks to a place where the independent church did not share the iconoclast doctrine.

Defeat of the declining Caliphate's Egyptian fleet in 965 ended the condominium. Without its constraints, the peasants, Christian and Moslem alike, found in the new Byzantine governors much harsher taskmasters and tax collectors.

## The Crusades

Cyprus became a key strategic post for Byzantine interests in Syria and Palestine. The governor organized protection for pilgrims to the highly dangerous Holy Land and supervised rebuilding of Jerusalem's Holy Sepulchre and fortifications for its Christian Quarter. The invasion of Ottoman Turks in Anatolia and the Levant after 1071 threatened communications with Constantinople, but Cyprus was still able to supply food to soldiers in the First Crusade of 1097 and even provided refuge for defeated Moslem princes.

The capital was established in the 12th century at the safer inland location of Nicosia. New trade developed with **17**

Venice and the young Crusader states on the mainland. With Salamis harbour silted up, port activities moved down the coast to Famagusta. Other main trading ports were now Limassol to the south and Kyrenia on the north coast.

The Turks' complete conquest of Anatolia in 1176 isolated Cyprus from the Byzantine government. Isaac Comnenius, a junior member of the imperial family, felt free to make himself 'Emperor' of Cyprus, using Sicilian mercenaries to fight off the Byzantine fleet. He ruled the island with brutal cruelty.

Salvation seemed to come in the form of England's Richard the Lionheart, who docked at Limassol on his way to the Crusades. He crushed the tyrant Isaac and was welcomed by cheering crowds in the streets of Nicosia. Isaac surrendered on condition that he would not be clamped into irons, so Richard clamped him into silver chains. Despite his English sense of humour, the Cypriots soon realized Richard was not altogether to be trusted. To pay for his expedition to the Holy Land, he stripped the island of all its money and Greek Cypriots were denied any governing role. They were ordered to shave off their beards, the supreme humiliation.

## Lusignans, Genoese and Venetians

After various dealings with knightly orders, Richard left the island in the hands of Guy de Lusignan, regarded by fellow Crusaders as *simplex et minor astutus*. This ex-king of

8-2012

*Tower (right) and fresco (below left) of a typical Limassol church.*

Jerusalem from French Poitou proved at least astute enough to bring barons in from war-torn Palestine with the promise of a safer life on Cyprus's fertile (and free) farm estates. The Lusignan dynasty's feudal rule reduced native Cypriots to serfdom. In 1260, the Roman Catholic Church was declared supreme on the island, but Orthodox priests remained the real spiritual authority inside the Greek-Cypriot community.

Originally Byzantine, the Crusaders' mountain redoubts at St Hilarion, Kantara and Buffavento set the pattern for the feudal castles of western Europe. Church architecture drew on French Gothic models for Nicosia's 13th-century St Sophia cathedral (now Selimiye mosque) and Bellapais Abbey near Kyrenia, and Rhineland Gothic for Fama-gusta's St Nicholas cathedral (now Lala Mustafa Pasha mosque).

In the 14th century, Cyprus profited greatly as a Christian outpost supplying the mainland Crusaders. Famagusta merchants were renowned for their extravagant luxury. In the mountains, the barons used leopards to hunt the island's coveted wild moufflon sheep. The island's opulence attracted pirates and a heated rivalry between the merchants of Genoa and **19**

Venice which erupted in bloody riots in 1345. The Cypriots sided with the stylish Venetians against the rapacious Genoese. Avenging the murder of its merchants and looting of its shops in Famagusta, Genoa sent a fleet to ravage the whole island. In 1374, the Genoese extorted reparations of 2 million gold florins and confiscated the port of Famagusta.

The Lusignan kings had become too fat and sluggish to resist Italian demands. James II needed help from the Sultan of Egypt to oust the Genoese in 1464, but the gold it cost him emptied his treasury. After his death, the Venetians stepped into the breach through James' widow, Queen Caterina Cornaro. After years of intrigue, they sent her back to Italy with a generous pension as golden handshake and ruled Cyprus for 82 years.

The Venetians' lucrative trade was threatened by Ottoman encroachment on three sides – Anatolia, the Levant and Egypt. In 1570, the Turks flatly demanded that they give up Cyprus. Imagining that attack would come from the east, the Venetians consolidated their defences mainly in Famagusta. But Lala Mustafa Pasha, governor of Damascus, landed on the south coast and headed inland to besiege the relatively lightly defended Nicosia, which fell after 46 days. The capital's Venetian commander was killed and his head sent to his counterpart at Famagusta as a warning. But Captain Marcantonio Bragadino led a heroic defence of the port city, 8,000 Greek-Cypriot and Italian troops holding out for over 10 months against a Turkish army of 200,000. On 1 August 1571, when the defenders were reduced to just 400 men, Bragadino surrendered. He was promised safe conduct but then flayed alive. Cyprus became a province of the Ottoman Empire.

## Turkish Rule

With the Turks controlling the whole of the eastern Mediterranean, Cyprus lost its strategic importance and was left to stagnate. Some 20,000 new settlers were brought in from Anatolia. The Turkish administrators, for the most part Nicosia-based tax collectors, proved more idle than oppressive. Roads, fortresses and churches fell into ruin. Just as mosques in Spain had been turned into cathedrals, so Gothic churches here were converted to mosques with an added minaret or two.

But after 250 years of Catholic intolerance, Greek Cypriots appreciated the regained status of the Orthodox Church. By 1660, the Sultan made their archbishop directly responsible for the Cypriot citizenry. He could and did appeal to the Sultan over the heads of local officials. This authority extended gradually from the people's personal needs to the collecting of taxes for the Ottoman treasury so as to counter the corrupt and often rebellious Turkish administrators. Peasants found taxes an ever heavier burden, but at least they could now shrug off feudal serfdom and acquire their own land.

For the archbishop's dealing with the Turkish authorities, a Greek-Cypriot interpreter or *dragoman* was appointed who could acquire great influence and wealth by playing off one side against the other. Archbishop and middleman were often suspected of exploiting their responsibility for the undue enrichment of the church or themselves. At the beginning of the 19th century, dragoman Hadjigeorgakis Kornessios was considered the wealthiest and most powerful man on the island. During the Greek War of Independence of 1821, Archbishop Kyprianos let Greek rebel ships pick up supplies on the north coast. Turkey immediately sent in 4,000 Syrian troops. The archbishop and three of his bishops were executed. More troops were brought in from Egypt, resulting in large-scale massacres and plunder of church property.

Over the next 50 years, the Sultan tried to halt widespread abuses by Turkish tax collectors which were provoking **21** massive emigration of Greek and Turkish Cypriots. Local Turkish officials opposed all reforms, often resorting to armed intimidation of governors sent in by the Sultan. The disintegration of Ottoman authority in Cyprus was symptomatic of the imminent collapse of the empire.

## The British Step In

With 'the sick man of Europe' on his deathbed, the superpowers of the time hovered around like vultures to pick at the remains, among which Cyprus was a choice little bone. Britain was concerned that the eastern Mediterranean remain safe for its ships to pass through the Suez Canal to India. To keep Russia out, Britain signed the Cyprus Convention with Turkey, whereby the island came under British administration while formally remaining the Sultan's possession. On 12 July 1878, the deal was sealed with a peaceful little flag-raising ceremony in Nicosia that contrasted sharply with the bloody massacres that had once heralded the arrival of the Crusaders or the Turks.

The British envisaged the island less as a military base than as a staging area to assemble troops in case of joint action with Turkey in the Caucasus or – over a century before the Gulf War was to activate the plan – in Mesopotamia (modern Iraq). But by 1882, Cyprus's strategic significance had been superseded by British occupation of Egypt, which provided Alexandria as direct protection for the Suez Canal. Only the first two British governors of Cyprus were military men. Thereafter, civilians from the Colonial Office did the job.

Greek Cypriots were happy about the transfer of power from corrupt Turks to upright Britons. They appreciated the new schools, hospitals, law courts and roads that had

**22**

*This church bonfire in the village of Kato Lefkara is an essential part of Easter celebrations.*

become the hallmark of British colonial administration. Population rose from 186,000 in 1881 to 310,000 in 1921. But the most important contribution they expected from the British would be to help Cyprus achieve union with Greece – *enosis* – as they had done for Corfu and the other Ionian Islands in 1864. As long as he was in opposition, Gladstone supported the claim, but did nothing about it when he became prime minister.

It was of course opposed by the Turkish-Cypriot minority – 46,500 (25%) in 1881. They usually remained calm, confident that Britain would respect its alliance with Turkey and not give in, but violent demonstrations did break out when the Greek-Cypriot *enosis* campaign grew vociferous.

In 1914, Turkey sided with Germany in World War I and Britain promptly annexed Cyprus. Turkey relinquished all claim after the Treaty of Lausanne in 1923 and the island became a British Crown Colony two years later.

More roads were built, but not in the direction of *enosis.* In 1931, impatient Greek-Cypriot members of the Legislative Council resigned, there were riots in Nicosia, a priest brandished the Greek flag crying 'I proclaim the revolution', and Government House was burned down. Troops were brought in from Egypt. Insurgent bishops were deported, political parties banned, the Greek flag outlawed and press censorship imposed. But in World War II, in response to the British alliance with Greece against Germany and Italy, Cypriots rallied to the British flag and furnished a 30,000-strong regiment. The island's political parties were duly reinstated.

## Fight For Identity

Britain's Labour government of 1945 thought it was doing Cyprus a favour by moving it, like other colonies, towards self-rule. But the slogan of the day was '*Enosis* and only *enosis*'. In 1950, the year that a plebiscite of Greek Cypriots voted 96% in favour of union with Greece, the Church appointed a new leader, Archbishop Makarios III.

In 1955, the campaign for *enosis* became an armed struggle led by Lieutenant-Colonel George Grivas, a Cypriot-born Greek Army officer. He was – and still is – known to Cypriots as Dighenis, a code name inspired by the legendary hero of an 11th-century Greek epic, Dighenis Akritas. The name means 'frontiersman born of two races', though the true *enosis*-fighter might claim that Cypriots and Greeks are the same race.

EOKA (Greek initials for the National Organization of Cypriot Struggle) had, unlike other anti-colonial movements of the time, a right-wing ideology with violent methods opposed by the island's leftist trade unions and Communist Party. Directed by Grivas from a hideout in the Troodos mountains, EOKA blew up public buildings and killed opponents of *enosis*. Makarios publicly disowned the actions but gave EOKA clandestine

### Small Nation's Great Leader

Cyprus was blessed with a first president of powerful intellect and spiritual authority. Born in 1913 in a poor peasant family in the Troodos mountains, Mihail Christedoulous Mouskos became a monk at the Kykko monastery. He studied at Athens and Boston, USA, from 1938 to 1948, when he returned to Cyprus to become Bishop of Kition (Larnaca).

Archbishop at the remarkably young age of 37, he won popular support with his dignified eloquence. But he was also criticized by foreign observers for his failure to control Greek-Cypriot extremists, thus provoking alarm in the Turkish-Cypriot community which might have been avoided. But he impressed the world with his moral leadership of non-aligned nations at the height of the Cold War and great physical courage during the Turkish invasion of 1974.

**25**

support. He was exiled in 1956, first to the Seychelles and then to Athens. The Greek public gave noisy support to the Greek-Cypriot cause, but their government was reticent.

Turkey backed Turkish-Cypriot opposition to *enosis* with two main arguments: the Moslem community would be defenceless if swallowed up in the greater Greek nation; and Greek extension to Cyprus would pose a direct military threat to Turkey. In 1958, Turkish Cypriots rioted in favour of partitioning the island.

In 1959, as guarantors (with the British), Turks and Greeks met in Zurich and agreed to renounce both *enosis* and partition, while guaranteeing strict safeguards for the Turkish-Cypriot minority. The president of the new independent republic would be Greek-Cypriot Archbishop Makarios, and his vice-president would be the Turkish-Cypriot leader, Fazil Kuchuk. On August 16, 1960, Cyprus became independent, within the British Commonwealth. (Britain retained two military bases –

British Sovereign Base Areas – on the south coast.) Grivas retired to Athens, unhappy with the outcome.

## Troubled Independence

The constitution proved too complex to work. Cabinet posts, parliamentary seats and civil service jobs were apportioned to Greek and Turkish Cypriots according to a ratio of 7 to 3 (the demographic ratio was 8 to 2). The main towns elected separate Greek- and Turkish-Cypriot municipal governments. To give Turkish Cypriots added protection, taxation was subject to special restrictions.

In 1963, Makarios proposed 13 simplifying amendments which Turkey promptly vetoed even before the Turkish-Cypriot leadership had voiced an opinion. Communal fighting broke out in Nicosia. the British supervised a ceasefire and set up a 'Green Line' separating the communities in the capital. United Nations forces were brought in to patrol it in March 1964, and have been there ever since.

Turkish-Cypriot enclaves were formed mainly in the northern part of the island. Turkey and Greece each sent in officers to train local forces.

In 1974, in a bid to regain popularity at home, Greece's military junta tried to impose *enosis* in Cyprus. Makarios resisted and demanded that the Greek officers be withdrawn from the island. The junta responded by engineering a military attack on the Presidential Palace in Nicosia. Makarios escaped to Paphos where he broadcast to the people of Cyprus refuting reports of his assassination. This *coup d'état* gave Turkey a pretext to invade. Within three weeks, Turkish troops had occupied most of northern Cyprus. Makarios escaped to New York where he rallied support in the United Nations to reinstate him as president. He died in 1977.

The Turkish army remained in control of 37% of the island, including Famagusta, northern Nicosia and Kyrenia. The troops have been accused of plundering churches, and Greek-Cypriot art treasures from the north have begun to appear on the international market. Some 170,000 Greek Cypriots were forced to flee to the south, while about 30,000 Turkish Cypriots migrated to the north. By 1992, some 80,000 new settlers had been brought into northern Cyprus from Turkish Anatolia.

In 1983, a 'Turkish Republic of Northern Cyprus' was set up under Rauf Denktash, but recognized only by Turkey. The UN Security Council has condemned the move and urged Greek-Cypriot President George Vassiliou and Denktash to find a way other than partition for protecting minority rights on the island. Because of its diplomatic isolation, the economy in northern Cyprus has stagnated badly. Greek Cypriots have recovered from the initial shock of invasion and their economy was thriving again by 1992, thanks in large part to tourism. But reunification with the north remains their national goal. **27**

# Where to Go

To help you plan your itinerary, we have divided the island into six sections. Wherever possible, one of the main cities is used as a base from which to make a series of day trips. Even if you are not actually staying overnight in the base-town, it is a good idea to get to it early in the morning for a comfortable day trip. The six sections are:

*Nicosia*, the lively, historic capital, with trips south to the ancient tombs of Tamassos, the monasteries of Ayio Herakleidos and Macheras; west into the mountains to see the famous frescoes of Assinou church;

*Larnaca*, port and resort, and points west to Hala Sultan Tekke's Moslem shrine, the great Byzantine church at Kiti, Stavrovouni monastery, the Stone Age settlement at Khirokitia, and the handicraft village of Lefkara; east out to the resort of Ayia Napa, the beaches at Protaras, and Dherinia to see across to Turkish-occupied Famagusta;

*Limassol*, proud and cosmopolitan port city, and west to the Crusaders' castle of Kolossi, the ancient Greek site of Kourion, and Aphrodite's birthplace; south to Akrotiri beaches and monastery, and a gourmet expedition east to Germasogeia;

*Troodos Mountains.* If you are not staying overnight in Troodos, the most convenient base is Limassol, within easy reach of the villages of Omodos and Platres, Troodos resort itself, Kakopetria, and west to Kykkos monastery and Cedar Valley;

*Paphos*, ancient capital and modern resort, and east to neighbouring Yeroskipos, north to the beaches of Coral Bay, Ayios Neophytos monastery, and mountain villages at the western end of the Troodos range – Fyti, Pano Panayia (birthplace of Archbishop Makarios') and Panayia Chrysorroyiatissa monastery and winery; and for walking tours of the Akamas peninsula;

*Northern Cyprus* – the starting-point for this area is

Nicosia from where you can go to the port of Famagusta, ancient Salamis, Kyrenia harbour resort, Bellapais abbey and Crusaders' castles such as St Hilarion.

Those wanting really to get to know Cyprus rather than just to soak up the sun on its beaches should plan to stay in more than one place. If your main destination is at one of the island's extremities – Paphos or Ayia Napa – it is particularly important to stay at another, more central, location such as Nicosia, Limassol or Larnaca.

When you are planning your travels, it is reassuring to know that it is very easy to get from one end to the other of the Mediterranean's third largest island, not least because of the excellent network of roads. Nicosia in the interior and the south-coast towns of Larnaca and Limassol are linked by motorways (express-

ways), which are constantly being extended. The coastal highways west to Paphos and east to Ayia Napa are also first rate. You will find unpaved roads only between the remotest mountain villages.

Our *Blueprint* section at the back of the book gives detailed information about the practical business of getting around.

Wherever possible, try to plan your trip with the special-

*Striking colour scheme for this typical house in Nicosia.*

events calendar listed in our *Festivals* section in mind (see p. 98). Limassol is the place to be if you are on the island for the pre-Lenten Carnival. The leading monasteries organize spectacular candlelight processions for Easter (check the Orthodox calendar) and grand pilgrimages on Assumption Day (August 15).

And wherever you choose to go, your path will be smoother if you take the trouble to learn just five words of Greek: *Kaliméra,* 'Good morning'; *Kalispéra,* 'Good afternoon'; *Kalinikta,* 'Good night'; *Parakaló,* 'Please' and *Efcharistó,* 'Thank you'.

# Nicosia

Amid the animated prosperity of the town's southern sector, it is easy to forget the stretches of wall and barbed wire that make the divided capital a reluctant successor to Berlin. Although you can visit it only as part of the Turkish-occupied zone (see p. 38), we **30** include northern Nicosia here

to maintain a sense of the town's single identity.

Nicosia (*Lefkosia* in Greek, *Lefkosha* in Turkish) is Cyprus's only inland city, with excellent hotel, restaurant, shopping and entertainment possibilities – while for tourists, Nicosia makes a good base for sightseeing excursions.

Nicosia's history goes back to Neolithic times. Situated near the ancient site of Ledra, today's city was founded in the 4th century BC by Lefkon, son of Ptolemy I of Egypt. The origins of the name Lefkosia are uncertain. It could have been inspired by Lefkon himself or by the word *lefki* ('popular' in Greek). With the arrival of the Lusignans in the 12th century AD, the city was dubbed Nicosie (transformed by the British into Nicosia).

When coastal towns like Paphos and Salamis came under attack in the early 7th century AD, the population shifted to the interior and Nicosia became the chief city of the island. Under the Lusignans, Nicosia evolved into a splendid capital city. From the

12th to the 15th centuries, Nicosia's golden age, castles, churches and monasteries in French Gothic style were constructed. Just prior to the Turkish invasion of 1570, Venetians built the massive defensive wall, which is still standing.

When the Ottoman Turks took over after a six-week siege, 20,000 citizens lost their lives. Resistance to Ottoman rule flared up into outright rebellion in 1821, but the Turks suppressed the revolt. Nicosia suffered an outbreak of cholera in 1835 and a disastrous fire in 1857. And the heaviest fighting of the 1974 Turkish invasion took place here (some old bombed buildings are still deserted or serve as warehouses). But the buoyant city has survived all that to retain fascinating architectural reminders of past rulers, whether Lusignan, Venetian, Turkish or British. Independence and the post-partition era have spawned an array of functional office blocks that do at least testify to the town's economic vigour.

### Getting Into Locked Churches

In small country villages, the church remains closed to protect its treasured icons and frescoes from thieves and vandals. If you cannot get into any of the churches we describe, the key is usually to be found with the local priest or at the nearest café. If the café owner does not have a key, he will probably know where you can get one.

## THE FORTIFICATIONS

The ramparts hurriedly built by the Venetians from 1567 to 1570 to fend off the Turks remain Nicosia's dominant feature. Indeed, with its 11 pointed bastions and three giant gateways, the wheel-shaped Renaissance fortification, some 5 km (nearly 3 miles) in length, has become the modern capital's distinctive logo, a symbol of its historic unity.

The gates bear the names of the three coastal cities to **31** which they led: Famagusta to the east, Kyrenia to the north and Paphos to the west (the two latter gates in the town's Turkish-Cypriot sector).

Originally the main entrance to the old city, the massive **Famagusta Gate** is a tunnel-like building all to itself. Handsomely restored as Greek-Cypriot Nicosia's **Cultural Centre**, the stone barrel vaults provide a splendid setting for concerts, plays and exhibitions of modern art. During the city's annual summer arts festival, an open-air theatre is installed in the adjacent moat.

Some bastions shelter municipal offices, while sections of the moat (not completed in time to keep out the Turks) now serve as public gardens, playgrounds and car parks.

## GREEK QUARTER

Today, most visitors to the old city enter through **Eleftheria** (Liberty) **Square**, where you will find the Municipal Library, the Central Post Office and the Town Hall – this last a fanciful colonnaded structure of 1930, renovated in 1952. From the square, **Ledra Street** leads through the thriving old part of town, thronged with shoppers looking for popularly priced goods. Explore the crowded alleyways and tiny streets lined with shops, cafés and food stands (which exude exotic odours), especially late in the day when the air is cooler.

The new **Leventis Municipal Museum**, 17 Hippocrates Street, presents a beautifully

---

### Korrekt Spelling

Cypriot signmakers very kindly trans-literate names from the Greek, but with glorious inconsistency. Sometimes you will see *Pafos*, more often *Paphos*, saints are variously presented as *Ayios* or *Agios*. We have tried to impose some order on our spelling, but where we fail, we are at least capturing the true spirit of the place – our main objective.

*Omerye Mosque with its soaring minaret began life as an Augustinian monastery.*

designed account of Nicosia's history (winning the European Museum of the Year award in 1991). In a fine 19th-century Neoclassical mansion, it traces the city's long story *in reverse*, from today's capital of the Republic back to British colonial days, to rule by the Turks, the Venetians, the Lusignans, its Byzantine era and ancient Greek origins. Exhibits include costumes, utensils, coins and ancient ceramics, but also a rare portrait of Caterina Cornaro and a King George VI Coronation tea mug.

Immediately to the south, the revived **Laiki Yitonia** (Popular Neighbourhood) re-creates the atmosphere of old

**33**

Nicosia. Buildings in traditional style – some restored, others specially constructed – house quaint boutiques, tavernas, flats and artisans' galleries (you can watch the craftsmen while they work), as well as an office of the Cyprus Tourism Organization.

Make your way east towards the minaret landmark of **Omerye Mosque,** transformed by the town's 16th-century Turkish conquerors from the Augustinian monastery church of St Mary's. Still used by the few hundred Moslem worshippers living in the Greek-Cypriot sector (mostly Arab students), it is also open to visitors wishing to climb the minaret's spiral stairway. It affords a great view across to the northern sector and beyond to the Kyrenia Mountains.

At 18 Patriarch Gregorios Street, the house of Hadji-geogakis Kornessios, **Konak Mansion**, is a beautiful 18th century structure with Gothic-style doorway and overhanging, closed balcony. Restored **34** to some of its original glory,

the interior is notable for the ornate stairway and the grand reception room's painted ceiling and opulent furnishings. They testify to the wealth accumulated by this go-between for the Turkish sultan and Cypriot archbishop.

## AROUND THE ARCHBISHOP'S PALACE

The Archbishop's Palace stands at the centre of much of the old city's cultural life. The **palace** itself (residence closed to visitors) is a fanciful modern pastiche of Venetian architecture. Amid the splendour of the state rooms, Archbishop Makarios III installed an austere bedroom with simple chest and iron bed, a humble resting place for the heart of the revered national leader.

Housed in a public wing of the palace, the **Byzantine Museum** has rescued and restored a superb collection of icons from all over the island. Presented with loving care and attention to lighting, they offer the full range of Byzantine art on Cyprus from a primitive

*The pseudo-Venetian Archbishop's Palace, with a monument to Archbishop Makarios III in the foreground.*

9th-century Virgin Mary to the decline in the 18th century. Highlights from the golden era of Cypriot art in the 12th century are a luminous Christ giving his blessing and a solemn Virgin and Child, both from Lagoudhera in the Troodos mountains.

Upstairs is a large collection of European paintings from the 16th to the 19th centuries. Attributions to the masters are doubtful, but it is worth testing the national Cypriot pulse with a look at local themes – noble Greek peasants and indolent Turkish pashas. Pride of place goes to *Massacre at Chios*, attributed variously to Delacroix or Courbet, both fervent champions of the Greek cause against the Turks.

Next to the museum, **Ayios Ioannis** (St John's) is Nicosia's Orthodox cathedral, built in 1665 in an approximation of Late Gothic style. The 18th-century frescoes depict landmarks in the island's early Christian history from the mission of Paul and Barnabas in AD 45 to the bestowal of imperial privileges on the Archbishop of Cyprus in 488.

The adjacent Gothic-arcaded monastery building is now the **Folk Art Museum**, displaying wooden water wheels, looms, pottery, carved and painted bridal chests, lace and embroidered costumes.

Opposite the nearby Pancyprian Gymnasium, a high school famous for its *enosis* activism in the 1950s, the **National Struggle Museum** documents the EOKA armed uprising against British rule in the 1950s. Revolutionary ardour is dimly recaptured by a collection of guns, hand-grenades, bayonets, old newspapers and the command-car of EOKA leader Griva Dighenis, a small burgundy-red Hillman.

## THE NEW TOWN

Outside the old walls, Nicosia's smarter shops and restaurants are to be found along Evagoras and Archbishop Makarios avenues, south of Elefthera Square.

### Traces of War

At the end of Ledra Street, and indeed any time you stray too far north, you will run into the Green Line barring entry to northern Nicosia. The border is usually marked by rolls of rusting barbed wire across overgrown no-man's-land, but also by an occasional stretch of wall, bizarrely adorned with camouflage paint, where United Nations troops mount somewhat lackadaisical guard at the command post. A few burned-out buildings in this border wasteland still bear witness to combat in the 1974 Turkish invasion.

A modern **Handicrafts Centre** lies south of the town centre on Athalassa Avenue. Artisans, many of them refugees from northern Cyprus, can be seen at work from 7.30 a.m. to 2 p.m. The products of their embroidery, weaving, wood-carving, pottery and leather-tooling are for sale. There is no pressure on you to buy, but the wares here are likely to be of better quality than in the usual souvenir shops.

Some of the best authentically Cypriot restaurants are to be found in the suburbs of **Strovolos** and **Engomi**.

## CYPRUS MUSEUM

The island's proud collection of antiquities is housed out on Museum Street just south of the Green Line, near the Turkish-Cypriot sector's old Paphos Gate. The sculpture, ceramics and jewellery here give you a fine insight into the unique Cypriot synthesis of Greek and Levantine culture. (Exhibits are constantly moved around. We present highlights in a chronological order which will not always correspond to their display.)

Exhibits of the Bronze Age include the some of the first implements made from the island's all-important copper mines, red-polished and white-painted pottery. Look for the clay bowl-shaped **sanctuary model** (2000 BC), in which worshippers and priests surround a bull sacrifice while a Peeping Tom on the sanctuary wall watches the secret ceremony.

An intriguing **Mycenaean krater** (drinking cup) imported to Enkomi by merchants from the Peloponnese in the 14th century BC has an octopus motif framing a scene of Zeus preparing warriors for battle at Troy. A **blue faïence rhyton** (ritual anointing vessel) (13th century BC, from Kition) depicts a lively bull-hunt – a Mycenaean theme, but the hunters are distinctly Syrian.

Fascinating **royal tomb-furniture** from Salamis (8th century BC) includes an ivory throne, a bed, a sword and the **37** remains of two chariots and their horses' skeletons.

A major highlight is the showcase displaying scores of **votive statues and figurines** (625 to 500 BC) Swedish excavators found 2,000 of them at Ayia Irini in north-west Cyprus, preserved just as they originally stood around an altar of an open-air sanctuary. In a dual cult of war and fertility, soldiers, war-chariots, priests with bull-masks, sphinxes, minotaurs and bulls were fashioned life-size or just 10 cm (4 in) tall, according to their ritual importance. Apparently of no great importance in those days are the shrine's only females, two small statuettes.

Lacking the more refined possibilities of marble on the island, Cypriot limestone sculpture tends to be psychologically inexpressive, with one magnificent exception, a poignant **woman's head** (3rd century BC) from the Aphrodite sanctuary at Arsos, north of Larnaca.

A true masterpiece of Roman-Cypriot art is the monumental bronze of **Emperor Septimius Severus** (*c*. AD 200) in heroic nudity despite his orator's pose.

(Outside, you can rest in the pleasant **Municipal Gardens** across the street, next to the Municipal Theatre.)

## TURKISH QUARTER

Visit the sights, mostly inside the old ramparts, as part of your tour of Northern Cyprus (see p. 87 for entrance requirements). From Kyrenia Gate, follow the avenue of the same name to **Mevlevi Tekke**, once a monastery inhabited by members of the whirling dervishes sect, outlawed in 1925. The 17th-century building with its several domes now houses a **Museum of Arts and Crafts**.

Brownstone government office buildings rim **Atatürk Square**, hub of the Turkish quarter. Here stands the post office and a granite column probably brought from Salamis by the Venetians. The Turks removed it when they conquered Cyprus in 1570, and it was re-erected in 1915. Unfortunately the St Mark's lion once crowning it disappeared, and the copper globe you see is a recent addition.

From Atatürk Square, Asmalti Street leads past a couple of old Turkish **inns** with picturesque courtyards and verandahs: Kumardjilar Khan (now restored) and Buyuk Khan. In the 18th century the Turks built these *khans* or *hans* as hospices for visiting foreigners. A main door gave onto a courtyard surrounded by rooms. Although the main door was bolted, a smaller door within it, called the 'eye of the needle', was left open for travellers – so that camels, carts and other conveyances could not enter.

With its minarets and lofty Gothic arches, **Selimiye Mosque**, formerly the great French Cathedral of St Sophia, is an eloquent landmark of the city's dual identity. The cathedral was begun in 1209 under the first Latin archbishop, Thierry, reaching completion in the 14th century. Here the Lusignan princes were crowned kings of Cyprus, and here Christian worship took place – until the Turks turned the church into a mosque following the 1570 conquest. Note the western façade and its porch with three portals surmounted by a rose window; with moulded ogival arches and carved figures of saints, royalty and clergy, this could be a cathedral transported straight from France.

The **Bedestan** or old market next door dates from the 12th to the 14th centuries, when it was constructed as the Church of St Nicholas-of-the-English. The Turks converted the church into a covered market – today disused. But you can still admire the carved Gothic doors, the family crests and religious sculptures above the main portal, the barrel-shaped roof, three apses and dome. In the crumblings interior are some wall paintings, notably one of St Andrew (12th century).

Also near the cathedral, the **Sultan's Library** preserves important books in Turkish, Arabic and Persian.

**39**

## AROUND NICOSIA

The following excursions are all within 50 km (30 miles) of Nicosia, making them easy day trips.

### Royal Tombs and Monasteries

Just over 12 km (7 miles) south-west of the capital, near the village of Politiko, is the site of **Tamassos**, ancient city-kingdom rich in copper. Archaeologists have uncovered a sanctuary and altar to Aphrodite. The **royal tombs** (6th century BC), with stairways and narrow dromos passages approaching the burial chamber, are carved in stone to imitate wooden dwellings, complete with simulated bolted doors, window sills and 'log-roof' ceilings.

The nearby **Monastery of Ayios Herakleidos** is now in the hands of nuns who tend the gardens and sell honey, marzipan and other sweetmeats. After many restorations, the present 18th-century structure houses, in a domed mausoleum, the remains of the saint who guided Paul and Barnabas on their mission to Cyprus. First bishop of Tamassos, Herakleidos was burned alive by unbelievers; his skull and a hand bone were salvaged and are now in a bejewelled gold reliquary.

Even unbelievers can enjoy the drive south-west past sweeping vistas of bleak valleys and wooded ravines to the **Monastery of Macheras**, 884 m (2,900 ft) up in the Troodos mountains. The region was a natural hide-out for EOKA second-in-command Gregoris Afxentiou, who died near the monastery in battle against the British in 1957. The monastery itself is a modern construction after an 1892 fire destroyed the original 12th-century foundation – its miracle-working icon of the Virgin Mary survived.

Down the road beyond Gourri, the village of **Phikardoú** represents a noble effort to sustain Cypriot rural traditions. It is protected as an Ancient Monument with a restoration programme for its subtly coloured ironstone houses and cobbled streets. The idea is not to create another folk museum, but to revitalize the community. At last count, in 1992, there were just 8 permanent residents (plus a dozen cats), though others may be enticed back by the handsome reconstruction. In the House of Katsinioros and House of Achilles Dimitri, you can see authentic old furnishings, a weaver's workshop, a wine press, a brandy still – and taste the results at the local taverna.

## Assinou Church

A second tour, some 30 km (19 miles) west of Nicosia, takes you past **Peristerona** to follow a sign-posted road to the hillside 12th-century church of Assinou, also known as Panayia Phorbiotissa. To view its magnificent Byzantine frescoes outside the holiday season, stop at the village of **Nikitari** to pick up the priest and keeper of the keys – remember to give him a small offering when you leave.

The modest but exquisite little church of ochre stone contains a veritable gallery of Byzantine art from the 12th to 16th centuries: a splendid *Pantocrator* (Christ in Majesty) in the narthex dome; a *Last Judgment* in which the damned seem at least destined for a more interesting time than the rather sad-looking heaven-bound blessed. Frescoes in the nave and bays depict the *Washing of the Feet, Raising of Lazarus, Crucifixion* and *Entombment*. But for a scene sublime beyond art, look back through the narthex to the frescoes framing the west door open to the green wooded slope beyond.

## Larnaca

The town is booming. It must be said that it has benefitted considerably from the 1974 partition. Its airport has replaced Nicosia's abandoned airfield as the Republic's international port of entry. The population has almost doubled since the influx of refugees, **41** mostly from Famagusta, the seaport is reviving. Beach resort facilities have burgeoned, the best out north around Larnaca Bay rather than downtown.

While its own cultural attractions are limited to the Pierides museum, St Lazarus Church and archaeological ruins of its origins, Larnaca makes a comfortable base for exploring the interior and coast of the island's south-east corner.

Much of northern Larnaca is built over the ancient city-kingdom of Kition (Kittim to the Turks). Legend attributes its founding to Kittim, a grandson of the Biblical Noah. Excavated traces of dwellings from the 2nd millennium BC make this the oldest continuously inhabited city of Cyprus. Mycenaean refugees from the Peloponnese arrived around 1200 BC. Three centuries later, enterprising Phoenicians took their place, prospering from the export of copper from Tamassos. But the city fell into decline after its alliance with Persia in the war with Athens (5th century BC). The Phoenician kingship came to an end in 312 BC.

The Lusignan barons revived the town as an important commercial and shipping centre. Because of the nearby salt

Cycling is still one of the best ways of getting around Larnaca.

lake, it was renamed Salina, the present name of Larnaca not catching on much before 1600. (Kition was retained as the name of the Orthodox diocese – Makarios was Bishop of Kition before becoming Archbishop of Cyprus.) Under the Turks, the foreign merchants who made it their home and the many consulates needed to protect their interests gave the town a cosmopolitan air quite lacking in Nicosia. In the 19th century, Famagusta took away much of Larnaca's commercial activity, but the 1974 partition has swung the pendulum back again to the island's south coast.

## THE SEAFRONT

The Foinikoudes (Palm Tree) Promenade changes its name from Athens Avenue to Ankara as its passes cafés and tavernas overlooking the pleasure boat marina and broad sandy beach. In the heart of what was the Turkish quarter, the avenue becomes Pyale Pasha from the corner dominated by the **Turkish Fort** (1605). View the harbour from the ramparts where cannons once fired (friendly) shots to salute passing ships. Inside the fort are a few archaeological finds from Kition and Hala Sultan Tekke (see p. 46), and stone inscriptions in both Arabic and Hebrew left by the Moslem and Jewish communities who once lived here side by side.

Across the street is the **Djami Kebir Mosque** founded in the late 16th century, serving now just a few Arab students and businessmen. Notice the beturbanned tombstones in the little corner graveyard, rare in such proximity to a mosque.

## CHURCH OF ST LAZARUS

A couple of blocks inland (at the end of Dionysou Street), you will see the three-tiered blind-arched campanile of the town's most revered church, dedicated to the man said to have sailed here after Jesus raised him from the dead. It was believed the man of **43**

Bethany became bishop of Kition before dying, this time for good. The church was erected over his tomb and rebuilt many times.

Its style is now an eclectic mixture of extravagant Byzantine, Romanesque and Gothic. On the iconostasis, the depictions of the raising of Lazarus include one in silver filigree in which a bystander is holding his nose, a popular feature in early representations of the miracle. In the crypt is the empty sarcophagus.

A small English cemetery to be found alongside the church contains marked graves of merchants, seamen and consuls from the days of the Ottoman Empire.

*A*n oasis in a desert of salt flats: Hala Sultan Tekke Shrine.

charming setting for hundreds of archaeological finds and works of art tracing Cypriot history from Neolithic to Byzantine times.

Highlights include: pottery of carved stone and red polished clay; expressive statuettes such as a chubby little terracotta fellow shouting his mystic anguish; idols of Astarte (Kition Phoenician counterpart to Aphrodite); mediaeval glazed ceramics; Roman glassware from 200 BC to AD 300; Cypriot embroidery, costumes and furniture – many of them Pierides family heirlooms.

North-west of the city centre, the **District Museum** stands at the corner of Kilkis and Kimon streets (near a cinema showing English-language films with a deafening sound system). Of principal interest here are the prehistoric finds from nearby

## THE MUSEUMS

Diagonally across from the tourist office, the **Pierides Museum** (Zeno Kitieos Street) draws on the private collection of the Swedish honorary consul, Demetrios Pierides (1811–95) and succeeding generations. The old family home provides a

Khirokitia (see p. 49) and Kalvasos and the excavations at Kition. The collection displays hoards of coins and jewels, ornaments, vases, lamps, tools and mirrors.

Signposted uphill beyond the District Museum, the **Kition Acropolis** (13th century BC) will appeal chiefly to seasoned archaeology buffs, but a boardwalk stroll through the site has its own surreal charm, hemmed in as it is by the surrounding houses' resolutely concrete-and-iron-rod modernity.

## WEST OF LARNACA

About 5 km (3 miles) from town, in the direction of the airport, the **Salt Lake** that was a source of the ancient town's renewed prosperity covers an area of some 6.5 sq km (2 sq miles). Lying 3 m (10 ft) below sea level, it is a true lake only in spring, when it dries up: each year the salt is collected at the end of July. In autumn and winter, thousands of migratory flamingoes pass through in a colourful cloud of pink, as they do at Akrotiri near Limassol.

**Hala Sultan Tekke**, a Muslim shrine, looks like a mirage in the dry summer season – thrusting its minaret through greenery over the blinding salt flats. An important Muslim pilgrimage place, the shrine contains the remains of the Prophet Mohammed's maternal aunt, Umm Haam (Foster Mother), known as Hala Sultan in Turkish. According to Muslim tradition, Umm Haram came to Cyprus with a party of Arab invaders in 647 AD. She fell from her mule near the Salt Lake, broke her neck and was buried there. The Turks built the mosque in her honour in 1816.

To enter, you leave your shoes at the door. The outer room has brightly painted octagonal columns and there is a women's gallery to the right. In the inner sanctuary, the guardian points out the trilithon structure above Umm Haram's grave – two enormous stones about 4.5 m (about 15 ft) high, covered with a meteorite that is said

*The atmospheric 11th-century church of Panayia Angelostikos at Kiti.*

to have come from Mecca. A legend relates that it hovered in the air by itself here for centuries.

A couple of miles further west is the village of **Kiti**. Its famous church, **Panayia Angelostikos** (Built by Angels), stands just north of the main crossroads. Domed and in golden stone, the present 11th-century edifice replaces a much earlier structure. At the entrance is the 14th-century chapel belonging to a rich mediaeval family, the Gibelets. But the outstanding feature of the church is the splendid early Byzantine **mosaic** in the apse, considered among the finest in Cyprus. Shown standing, the Virgin Mary holds the Christ Child, flanked by the archangels Michael and Gabriel. **47**

At an altitude of about 730 m (2,400 ft), **Lefkara** – 50 km (30 miles) from Larnaca – is actually two villages, Pano Lefkara and Kato Lefkara, which occupy a picturesque site in the foothills of the Troodos mountains. The name Lefkara is synonymous with drawn embroidery (*lefkaritika*), the traditional cottage industry that has brought the village fame for over five centuries. Widely and wrongly known as lace, *lefkaritika* is linen openwork stitched with intricate geometric patterns.

Women still work in narrow streets and courtyards, patiently turning out embroidered articles. Most of them sell their work to one of four

*L*egend has it that Leonardo da Vinci visited picturesque Pano Lefkara to buy lefkaritika for the altar cloth of Milan Cathedral.

major companies in Lefkara, so you can't exactly pluck a doily from the hands of the maker. But *lefkaritika* is readily available in shops here and all over Cyprus. You can also buy delicious Turkish delight and figs here.

Just south is **Khirokitia**, a small village known mainly for its **Neolithic ruins**. One of the oldest sites in Cyprus, dating from 7000 BC, it was discovered in 1934 by Porfyrios Dikeos, then director of the Cyprus Museum. After a climb up some steep steps – on the other side of a bridge from today's town – visitors reach the most interesting of four areas. There is a main street and the stone foundations of beehive-shaped houses (*tholos*). Made of clay or mud bricks, the dwellings were built in successive layers; when a structure fell down, a new one was put up to take its place The dead were buried right in the cellar, so to speak: 26 skeletons were found in the ruins of one house. Among thousands of artefacts uncovered, many of

interest (tools, idols, beads) are exhibited in Nicosia's Cyprus Museum.

On the way back to Larnaca, make a detour to **Stavrovouni** (Mountain of the Cross), a hill-top monastery at an altitude of 689 m (2,260 ft). It affords a magnificent view north across Nicosia and the plain to the blue Kyrenia Mountains beyond and south over neatly terraced hills to the Salt Lake, Larnaca and the Mediterranean. Stavrovouni is built on the site of a shrine to Aphrodite which, like the monastery today, was off-limits to women. Nevertheless, Helena, mother of Emperor Constantine, is said to have ventured up there to found the monastery with a piece of the True Cross in AD 330 (see p. 15). Men are allowed to stay overnight in the austere monastic accommodation.

## EAST OF LARNACA

The island's south-east corner is its vegetable garden. Its potatoes, aubergines, tomatoes, cucumbers and onions **49** are all important produce for export. But here, too, the politico-military realities of Cyprus become most apparent. Just beyond the Larnaca Bay resort hotels, you pass through the British 'Sovereign Base Area' of **Dhekelia**. The Greek-Cypriot Republic is squeezed here into a narrow strip by the nearby border of the Turkish-occupied zone, swooping south to include Famagusta.

Close to the border, the village of **Pyla** claims the distinction of being the only community in which Greek- and Turkish-Cypriots still live side by side. It also boasts a mediaeval tower and some good fish restaurants.

With the Turkish occupation of Famagusta, **Ayia Napa** has been transformed from a tiny fishing village into a major seaside resort. Its beaches of fine sand, a rarity in Cyprus, have proved a huge commercial asset. Boutiques, cafés, restaurants and travel agencies have completely hemmed in the venerable **Monastery of Ayia Napa** (Our Lady of the Forest). Built around 1530, originally as a nunnery, it remains one of the island's handsomest surviving Venetian buildings. Seek out a moment of tranquillity in its Gothic cloister and interior courtyard with a charming octagonal marble fountain. Carved out of the rock, the

---

### There Will Always Be A Corner

The two military bases at Dhekelia and Akrotiri are the last vestiges of Britain's empire in the Mediterranean. Reviving the Colonial Office's original concept for Cyprus back in 1878, they served as staging areas for the Persian Gulf in 1991 in the war against Iraq. Driving past today, notice Dhekelia's street-names recalling earlier campaigns, from Mandalay via Waterloo all the way back to Agincourt, with Knightsbridge Road thrown in presumably for ladies who fought at Harrods' sales.

*Domed fountain at the tranquil Ayia Napa monastery.*

church lies partially undergound. From the small chapel to the east, steps descend to an ancient sycamore said to be 600 years old.

At the island's south-eastern tip, **Cape Greco** presents spectacular rocky coves for hardy bathers seeking to escape the crowd. Families head for the sandy beaches at **Fig Tree Bay** and **Protaras**. The highway continues north to the resort of **Paralimnia**. It ends at the border town of **Dherinia**, where UN troops man a guard-post and homesick Greek-Cypriot refugees come for a roof-top view across to Famagusta.

# Limassol

When it comes to good living, the people of Limassol seem to consider themselves a cut above the rest of the island. These natural extroverts find the citizenry of Nicosia straitlaced, Famagustans, even in exile, too businesslike. Certainly, Limassol can boast particularly good restaurants, a brash and boisterous nightlife and it plays host to the island's wildest pre-Lenten Carnival.

A major role in all this is played by the big Cypriot wineries, all headquartered here. During the September wine festival, they offer complimentary samples of their wares and turn the local park into a free-wheeling open-air wine-bar.

The Limassol urban area was apparently occupied by small settlements from 2,000 BC onwards. But the town itself was of little importance before the Christian era and the time of the crusades, around the 12th century. The main centres of antiquity had been the city-kingdoms of **51**

Amathus to the east, now just a heap of ancient rocks, and Curium (Kourion) to the west, still a place of interest to tourists. Hence, the probable origin of the name Limassol, conjectured to be a corruption of Nemesos, Greek for 'in between' (the two ancient centres), which later became Lemesos and then Limassol.

It was here that England's Richard the Lionheart, leading a Crusade to Jerusalem in 1191, stopped off with his fiancée Berengaria. Badly received by the tyrant Isaac Comnenius, he took the island away from him and sold it – first to the Knights Templar (who settled in Limassol) and then to the Lusignans (see p. 18). Other Crusaders, the Knights of St John, settled in Limassol in 1291 and the town flourished as never before.

But the repeated natural calamity of earthquakes and the human rapacity of Genoese, Egyptians and Turks reduced the city by the early 19th century to a crumbling village. Development of the wine industry under the British

breathed new life into the place. Since the 1974 partition, Limassol's population has increased by 50% to nearly 125,000, second only to that of Nicosia. Besides refugees from the north, it counts a notable community of Lebanese and other, mostly prosperous immigrants from the Near East.

## INSIDE THE CITY

With only a few historic or cultural sights, the town's good resort hotels and nightlife nevertheless make it an attractive base from which to explore the outstanding archaeological sites to the west and the Troodos mountain villages to the north. The solitary monument to the town's feudal glory – the rest have succumbed to earthquake and enemy fire – is the **Castle**, just a few steps inland from the old port and customs house. The imposing stone fortification dates from the 13th century. Both the Lusignans and Venetians strengthened this ancient redoubt, which served the

*Hunt down a bargain amongst the street vendors in the old port area of Limassol.*

Turks as well after their conquest of Cyprus in 1571. In a pleasant tropical-greenery setting, it is surrounded by narrow lanes lined with artisans' shops, where the speciality is metalware (copper and tin), and where the craftsmen are bemused rather than amused by tourists.

The well-preserved castle contains a **mediaeval museum** displaying tombstones and weapons as well as photos of early Christian churches and medieval buildings from all over the island. The Gothic Great Hall, converted for use as a church and then a prison, has been restored. The prison **53** now seems a cosy place, with eight cells in pristine white limestone.

The small, modern **Limassol Museum** in Byron Street behind the Public Gardens contains some fascinating archaeological treasures. From shards and tools of Neolithic and Chalcolithic vintage, you'll progress through ceramics of the Bronze and Iron ages, with plenty of pottery right up through the Graeco-Roman period (plus coins, rings and other artefacts).

Don't miss the display of jewellery from various periods and the expressive terracotta figurines; one fat lady with a basket looks like a friendly old-fashioned washerwoman, while bulls and outsize dogs complete the amusing statuette scene. There's a beautiful head of Aphrodite from nearby Curium; a headless statue of a youth holding a bird (7th–6th century BC); some funerary steles; and a massive statue of the Egyptian god Bes – indeed an ugly fellow – found on the site of ancient Amathus in 1978.

The **Folk Art Museum**, 253 Ayios Andreas Street, provides a glimpse of rural Cypriot life, wood-carving, embroidery, jewellery and weaving – all coming together nicely in the display of a bride's robes and the elaborately carved chest for the finery of her trousseau.

As wine-making is not only an industry but also a tourist attraction, you'll find a visit to a **winery** both instructive and fun. On the outskirts of town, the top houses – Kep, Sodap and Etko – all offer short tours of their plant. You can see Cypriot wines, beers and spirits made and bottled – with a chance to taste. Tours usually begin around 10 a.m.

## AROUND LIMASSOL

East of town, hidden among the beach resort hotels, are the fenced-off ruins of **Amathus**, really of interest only to archaeological experts. Just north of Limassol is the little village of **Germasogeia**, reputed for its excellent tavernas in a pretty rural setting of the

Troodos foothills. On the outskirts is a picturesque dam where you can, with a licence, go fishing (see p. 92).

The coast road west past the wineries takes you along a delightful shady avenue that is a veritable arbour of eucalyptus and cypress trees bordered on either side by orange, lemon and grapefruit orchards.

## Akrotiri Peninsula

It was here that the traces of hunters of pigmy hippos, the earliest human presence on the island, were found (8500 BC). Half of the peninsula is **salt lake** – more flats than lake – popular with migratory birds, notably pink flamingoes from October to March. Most of the rest is occupied by the British 'Sovereign Base Area'. The peninsula's popularity with the British army is attested by a stretch of beach east of the salt flats known as Lady's Mile, after the colonel's mare that was brought here for a daily canter.

Just south of **Akrotiri** village, look for a track leading

*The four-square keep of Kolossi castle is one of the most striking examples of medieval architecture in Cyprus.*

east to **St Nicholas of the Cats Monastery**, a Gothic ruin on the site where the monks reared their special breed of anti-viper cats (see p. 16).

On the west side of the peninsula, **Kolossi Castle** is an impressive 15th-century keep jutting up out of gently rolling countryside. It was the headquarters of the Knights of St John of Jerusalem for administering their considerable sugar plantations and extensive vineyards. The *Comman-* **55** *derie,* as the headquarters were known, gave its name to their prized Commandaria sweet red dessert wine.

A stone stairway leads across the moat to the entrance. On your way in, notice the *fleur-de-lys* escutcheon over the east side entry, coat of arms of Louis de Magnac, Lusignan Grand Commander of the Order of St John. Among the spacious rooms with massive walls 3 m (10 ft) thick, the one with a huge walk-in fireplace was the kitchen. Climb the steep and narrow spiral staircase for the view from the battlements.

Outside you can see traces of an ancient aqueduct. Across from the keep, the imposing stone Gothic structure served as the Knights' sugar refinery.

## Kourion

Before exploring the great archaeological site itself, stop off in the nearby village of **Episkopi** to visit the fine little **Kourion Museum**. Founded in the 1930s by an American scholar who assembled objects he had excavated in the area, it now also holds dramatic recent finds from the earthquake that devastated Kourion in AD 365. On display is a group of three human skeletons, a 25-year-old male protecting a 19-year-old female with an 18-month-old baby clutched to her breast. Among the other exhibits from Kourion and the temple of Apollo are sculptures, a Roman stone lion fountain, terracotta vases and figurines

Just west of Episkopi, Kourion is – with Salamis in Northern Cyprus – the most important archaeological site on the island. Remains of its various settlements include a Greek temple, houses with superb mosaics, a theatre and stadium of the Roman era, and an early Christian cathedral. Not the least of its attractions is the site's spectacular view from a bluff high above Episkopi Bay. (In ancient times, sacrilegious criminals were hurled to their death on the rocks below.)

The area was inhabited back in the Stone Age, but

*Visitors to the Roman theatre at Kourion can enjoy superb views from the top of its steep steps.*

current historical opinion attributes the town's foundation to Mycenaean settlers in the 13th century BC. Known as Curium to the Romans, it converted to Christianity in the 4th century AD, faith sorely tested by a devastating earthquake in 365. After Arab raids in the 7th century, the bish-opric moved out to what is now Episkopi, leaving Kourion to sink into oblivion.

On the left as you enter the site (before reaching the tourist pavilion) are the fenced-in ruins of a colonnaded portico paved with an **Achilles Mosaic** (4th century AD). It depicts Achilles, dis- **57** guised as a woman to avoid enlistment in the Trojan army tricked by Odysseus into grabbing a spear and shield and revealing his true identity. The **House of Gladiators** nearby is so named for its beautifully coloured **mosaics** of two duels, one with a very aristocratic-looking referee – perhaps the owner of the house. (If closed, the guardian usually has the key.)

Beyond the main entrance gate (where guide maps to the site are on sale) are the remains of the **early Christian cathedral.** Approaching from the west, you pass the deacon's offices where a Greek inscription from the Psalms suggests that worshippers made their donations – 'Vow and pay to the Lord'. The plan of the basilica reveals 12 pairs of granite columns for the nave. Over to the left (north) is the **baptistery** with a dressing-room where people undressed for anointment with oil before descending to the cross-shaped font.

Continue on to the reconstructed **Roman theatre** (AD 50 to 175), which occupies a spectacular sloping site on the edge of the bluff. The auditorium housed 3,500 (and is back in use now for open-air performances). At the end of the 2nd century AD, the theatre spiced up its show with hunters pursuing and killing or being killed by wild animals. When you descend to the semi-circular orchestra, notice how the front rows were levelled to move spectators back to a safe distance.

Behind the theatre is the Roman **Villa of Eustolios**, started about AD 400. He must have been a fine fellow, this Eustolios, welcoming visitors with an inscription 'Enter ... and good luck to the house'. **Mosaics** of birds and fish indicate a man of wealth and taste. Inscriptions to Apollo and Jesus Christ suggest that religiously he was hedging his bets. He later added onto the villa a public bath house and health club. The **baths** are up a few steps. In the central room, notice some more remarkable mosaics, including one of a partridge, another of Ktisis, a deity personifying creation. She holds what seems to be a one-foot ruler, symbol of her function.

Back on the highway, about 1 km (½ mile) west of the main site, is the **stadium** (2nd century AD) where you can imagine athletics performed on the U-shaped track before some 6,000 spectators.

Continue west to the **Sanctuary of Apollo Hylates** (God of the Woodland), situated back from the highway in what was originally a deer forest and is now a charming setting of pines and evergreen scrub forest. Apollo was worshipped here from the 8th century BC but most of the present structures were put up around AD 100 and toppled by the great earthquake of 365.

From the guardian's lodge, take the path west to the pilgrims' entrance through **Paphos Gate.** The buildings here were probably hostels and storehouses for worshippers' votive offerings. The surplus was carefully placed in the *vothros* pit (at the centre of the site), which was full of terracotta figurines, mostly horse riders still intact

---

**The Honorary Consul**

Luigi Palma di Cesnola had the perfect front. In 1864, the Americans made him honorary consul-general in Larnaca, unperturbed by the fact that he was doing the same job simultaneously for the Russians. And when gold and silver antiquities came on the market which Luigi said he had dug up in Kourion in 1876, curators at New York's Metropolitan Museum rubbed their hands, paid the price and have proudly exhibited the 'Curium Treasure' ever since. Now international archaeologists agree that the treasure is in fact the loot from ancient tombs all over the island, systematically plundered throughout the years of his consular service. Investigators discovered no spade had ever dug into the site Luigi claimed he had excavated at Kourion.

when uncovered by the archaeologists. From here, follow the pilgrims' way along the sanctuary's main street north to a flight of stairs leading to the **Temple of Apollo**. It has been partially reconstructed, with simplified Corinthian capitals on its columns, as it appeared in AD 100.

Take the winding cliff road past vineyards to end your excursion at **Petra tou Romiou**, 46 km (28 miles) from Limassol, Aphrodite's legendary birthplace.

*Scenic contrasts: popular swimming spot near the Baths of Aphrodite (below) and the forests of Troodos (right).*

# Troodos Mountains

The Troodos chain in west-central Cyprus is the island's principal uplands and provides most of its fresh water and what the British Empire in its tropical outposts termed hill-stations, resorts where people can come up from the hot, arid plains to cool off amid the mountain greenery. The roads climb through foothills with rushing streams and orchards past villages perched on the slopes surrounded at higher altitudes by pine forest. Monks – and EOKA fighters – have found refuge here, and the monasteries are now joined by resort hotels and spas, with even a little winter skiing at the town of Troodos itself.

## PLATRES TO TROODOS

About 45 minutes from Limassol, 90 minutes from Nicosia, Pano Platres at 1,128 m (3,700 ft) makes an ideal base for visiting the whole Troodos region. With its hotels, restaurants and craftware shops,

the little town occupies a charming and shady mountain site. In high season, you will be joined by the bourgeoisie of Limassol whose summer homes swell the population from 500 to over 1,500. The Platres Festival of the folk arts is a major attraction.

The most popular sport is walking. (Even if an occasional snake may cross your path, only one in a hundred has a remotely harmful bite.) There is an easy 30-minute stroll via a trout farm at **Psilon Dhendron** over to the pretty little **Caledonian Falls**. The hardier rambler may carry on for another 60 minutes along a nature trail through the evergreen forest up to Troodos (see p. 62)

A short drive west of Platres is the friendly little village of **Phini**. With luck, the fine but higgledy-piggledy folklore museum may be open. In any case, have a coffee with the locals and then follow a hand-lettered sign up to the home of the local potter. Together with her whole family, the lady makes traditional Cypriot red- **61** clay ceramics and will be happy to let you watch them work.

**Troodhitissa Monastery**, 8 km (5 miles) to the north, was founded in the 13th century by a couple of hermits who had a vision in a nearby cave. Their church was twice destroyed by fire and the new one was built in 1731, with modern accommodation for guests. The silver-encased icon of the Virgin Mary and a holy leather belt *(ayia zoni)* with fertility powers for barren women attract considerable crowds on 15 August (Assumption Day).

Just 8 km (5 miles) uphill from Platres, the little resort town of **Troodos** is, at 1,676 m (5,500 ft) the island's highest resort, high enough to provide some decent skiing slopes in the winter. In summer, it offers a few tennis courts – and a tournament – and at weekends a lively throng of day trippers along its 'Main Street' stalls, shops and cafés. Ramblers tackle stark mountain trails through the forests of great twisted Aleppo pine struggling up out of the reddish clay and rocky cliffs. Armchair mountaineers may prefer to drive up above the town Cyprus's tallest peak, **Mount Olympus**, 1,951 m (6,401 ft). Ignore the giant 'golf ball' radar installation on the summit and, if visibility allows, look out over the length and breadth of the whole island.

## KAKOPETRIA

This is a favourite resort for Nicosians. If you are coming from the capital, continue on from your trip to Assinou (see p. 41). In the old part of town overlooking the ancient wooden flour mill, the balconied houses are being beautifully restored to bring out the subtle russet, amber and silver hues of the local stone.

Visit the nearby monastery church of **St Nicholas of the Roof** *(Ayios Nikolaos tis Steyis)*. An upper roof of shingles was built in the 13th century to shelter the older domed roof of tiles. Inside, its oldest **frescoes** date from the church's foundation in the 11th century, notably a *Raising of Lazarus* and the *Transfiguration*. Note, too, the highly expressive *Nativity*, *Entry into Jerusalem* and *Crucifixion*, all from the 14th century when Byzantine formal rigidity was breaking down.

## WEST TO KYKKO AND CEDAR VALLEY

The road west from Troodos winds through pine groves, vineyards and orchards of apples, pears, peaches, cherries, almonds and walnuts to **Prodhromos**, 1,402 m (4,600 ft) above sea level. The modest hotels and restaurants are popular with hikers. It has a highly respected Forestry College and you can visit the experimental orchard at **Trikouchia**, where new varieties of fruit are cultivated.

Further downhill is **Pedhoulas**, famous for its cherries and a popular destination in spring for Cypriots who flock to see the thousands of trees in blossom. Below the main church, the smaller, 15th-century **Archangel Michael Church** occupies an impressive site on a steep hill overlooking the valley. The most remarkable of its frescoes is a fierce representation of Michael himself. A giant cedar tree in the village centre is estimated by the Forestry Department to be over 450 years old – as a priest remarked, 'sprouting in the blessed days before the fall of Constantinople'.

Some 20 km (12 miles) from Pedhoulas, **Kykko Monastery** sits proudly remote from the world on a mountainside surrounded by pine forest. It is the island's most important pilgrimage monastery and included Archbishop Makarios among its novices. (It was also reputed to have served as a communications and supply base for the EOKA movement in the 1950s.) Founded in 1094 by a hermit, it grew in prestige when Emperor Alexis Comnenos gave it a rich land grant and an icon of the Virgin Mary said to have been painted by St. Luke. The icon survived several fires and is now **63** covered in gilded silver. Its legendary rain-making powers still bring in farmers to pray with the monks in time of drought. Today's buildings are bright and modern for the reception of pilgrims, particularly numerous at weekends for mass baptisms. By the hallowed icon of the Virgin Mary, offerings range from expensive jewellery to simple ex votos of beeswax. Outside, dozens of knick-knack stands line the way to a pleaseant café terrace.

Uphill beyond the monastery is the **Tomb of Archbishop Makarios**. In a site he chose long before his death, the venerated national leader is buried in a stylized cave-tomb watched over by an honour guard of the Cypriot army.

Home of the moufflon mountain sheep and a broad grove of cedar trees, **Cedar Valley** lies 14 km (9 miles) west of Kykko. Despite the unpaved road, it is worth the ride. Together with the Aleppo pine, plane and gold oak, the cedars make it a delightful setting for a hike or picnic. The valley boasts some 50,000 majestic specimens of the variety *Cedrus brevifolia* which the island shares with its neighbour, Lebanon. The oldest here, says the Forestry Department, dates back 850 years and stands 30 m (100 ft) tall.

*The inner courtyard of the remote – yet influential – Kykko Monastery.*

## Recommended Hotels

We give below a selection of hotels in three price categories, grouped in five resort areas: Nicosia, Limassol, Larnaca, Paphos and Ayia Napa. Prices will of course vary according to season, travel agent's package and unpredictable inflation. For booking directly with the hotel, we have included phone and, wherever possible, fax numbers.

All have air-conditioning and restaurant unless otherwise stated; 'beachfront' means directly on the beach. As a basic guide to room prices, we have used the following symbols (double occupancy with bath, including breakfast):

▌ below CY£36

▌▌ CY£36–60

▌▌▌ above CY£60

# NICOSIA
*(international tel/fax code 357.2)*

### Cyprus Hilton ▌▌▌
*Archbishop Makarios Ave.*
Tel. 46 40 40, fax 45 31 91
Luxury hotel set back from main road, 224 rooms, modern conference rooms, three restaurants, baby-sitting facilities, swimming pool, health club, tennis, boutiques.

### Kennedy ▌▌
*70 Regaena St.*
Tel. 47 51 31, fax 47 33 37
Friendly place inside old city walls, 92 rooms, baby-sitting service.

### Ledra ▌▌
*Grivas Dhigenis Ave, Engomi.*
Tel. 35 20 86, fax 35 19 18
Well-run modern hotel, quietly located, 5-minute ride from city centre, 103 rooms, conference facilities, tennis, swimming pool, boutiques.

## Nicosia Palace ▌
*4–6 C.Pantelides Ave.*
*Tel. 46 37 18*
Family bed and breakfast, nicely situated inside old city walls, baby-sitting service, not all rooms air-conditioned.

# LIMASSOL
*(international tel/fax code 357.5)*

## Alasia ▌
*1 Haydari St. Tel. 33 20 00, fax 33 54 25*
Hospitable traditional family hotel, swimming pool, tennis, baby-sitting service.

## Amathus Beach ▌▌▌
*Amathus, PO Box 513.*
*Tel. 32 11 52, fax 32 93 43*
Spacious luxury beachfront hotel 9 km (6 miles) east of city centre, 244 rooms, two swimming pools, tennis and other sports facilities, live music entertainment.

## Ariadne ▌▌
*28th October Ave.*
*Tel. 35 96 66, fax 35 74 21*
Friendly seafront family hotel, 70 rooms, swimming pool.

## Kanika Beach ▌
*28th October Ave.*
*Tel. 35 60 00, fax 35 21 24*
Well-equipped seafront hotel near city park, boutiques, swimming pool, tennis and other sports facilities.

## King Richard ▌
*Amathus, PO Box 4410.*
*Tel. 32 13 30, fax 32 10 57*
Cheerful seafront hotel 8 km (5 miles) east of Limassol, swimming pool.

# LARNACA
*(international tel/fax code 357.4)*

## Beau Rivage ▌
*Larnaca–Dhekelia Rd.*
*Tel. 62 36 00, fax 65 68 04*
Large well-run beachfront hotel east of town, 188 rooms, swimming pool, tennis and other sports facilities.

## Flamingo Beach ▌
*Piale Pasha St. Tel. 62 16 21, fax 65 67 32*
Family seafront hotel on southern edge of town, 64 rooms, swimming pool.

**67**

### Golden Bay ▐ ▐ ▐
*Larnaca–Dhekelia Rd.*
*Tel. 62 34 44, fax 62 34 51*
Luxury beachfront hotel east of town, swimming pool, tennis and other sports facilities, live music entertainment.

### Karpasiana Beach ▐ ▐
*Larnaca–Dhekelia Rd.*
*Tel. 65 50 01, fax 64 42 43*
Lively beachfront hotel on Larnaca Bay east of town, 105 rooms, swimming pool, tennis and other sports facilities.

### Sandy Beach ▐ ▐
*Larnaca–Dhekelia Rd.*
*Tel. 62 43 33, fax 65 69 00*
Friendly, large beachfront hotel on Larnaca Bay east of town, indoor and outdoor swimming pools, tennis and other sports facilities, live music entertainment.

### Sun Hall ▐ ▐
*Athens Ave.*
*Tel 65 33 41, fax 65 2717*
Seafront location convenient for city shopping and museums, 112 rooms, boutiques, conference rooms.

# PAPHOS & Region

*(international tel/fax code 357.6)*

### Annabelle ▐ ▐ ▐
*Poseidon St.*
*Tel. 23 83 33, fax 24 55 02*
Refined luxury beachfront hotel, close to harbour, 198 rooms, swimming pool, tennis and other sports facilities, boutiques, live music entertainment.

### Cynthiana Beach ▐
*Off Coral Bay Rd, PO Box 23.*
*Tel. 23 39 00, fax 24 46 48*
Big beachfront hotel 8 km (5 miles) north of town, 198 rooms, boutiques, swimming pool, tennis and other sports facilities, live music entertainment.

### Paphian Bay ▐ ▐
*Poseidon St. Tel. 24 33 33, fax 24 48 70*
Big beachfront hotel 5-minute ride south of town. Swimming pool, tennis and other sports facilities, live music entertainment.

## Roman  ▌▌

*Ayios Lambrianos St.*
*Tel. 24 54 11, fax 24 67 77*

Fanciful but tasteful 'ancient Roman' décor (mosaics, etc.), 68 rooms, swimming pool, boutiques.

## Marion  ▌

*Polis, PO Box 29.*
*Tel. 32 12 16, fax 32 14 59*

Convenient for Akamas Peninsula, 57 rooms, swimming pool, tennis.

## G & P Latchi  ▌

*Latchi. Tel. 32 14 11*

Modest, but ideal water-sports base, beachfront bed and breakfast, 9 rooms.

# AYIA NAPA & Region

*(international tel/fax code 357.3)*

## Asterias Beach  ▌▌

*PO Box 87.*
*Tel. 72 19 01, fax 72 20 95*

Large well-equipped beachfront hotel, swimming pool, tennis, boutiques.

## Cornelia  ▌

*PO Box 11.*
*Tel. 72 14 06, fax 72 24 09*

Small bed and breakfast, 28 rooms, swimming pool, air conditioning extra.

## Cristalla Protaras  ▌

*Protaras, PO Box 273.*
*Tel. 83 14 60, fax 83 15 84*

Small friendly family hotel, air conditioning extra, swimming pool.

## Grecian Bay  ▌▌▌

*PO Box 6.*
*Tel. 72 13 01, fax 72 13 07*

Giant luxury beachfront hotel, 271 rooms, indoor and outdoor swimming pools, tennis and other sports facilities, boutiques, live music entertainment.

## Tsokkas Protaras  ▌▌

*Protaras, PO Box 43.*
*Tel. 83 13 63, fax 83 14 47*

Large seafront hotel, swimming pool, tennis and other sports facilities, boutiques, live music entertainment.

69

# Recommended Restaurants

We appreciated the food and service in the restaurants listed below; if you find other places worth recommending, we would be pleased to hear from you. Our choices concentrate on restaurants and tavernas serving local cuisine rather than the easy-to-find 'international' places, pizzerias, fish-and-chip shops and other fast-food outlets. Some restaurants close one day a week, which may vary in and out of season, so call to confirm. Many taverns are open only for dinner.

Apart from a few pretentious establishments and luxury hotel-restaurants (none of which we have included here), average meal prices (starter, main course and dessert) are remarkably uniform, CY£4–7 per adult, depending on drinks. Our symbols rate cuisine, ambience and service:

‖ fair      ‖‖ good      ‖‖‖ excellent

# NICOSIA

### Aegeon   ‖

*40 Hector St. Tel. 43 04 54*

Combined with a bookshop, a favoured spot for Nicosia artists and intellectuals in old city near Famagusta Gate. Dinner only.

### Kavouri   ‖‖

*125 Strovolos Ave, Strovolos. Tel. 42 51 53*

Good fish taverna worth the short trip to the south-west outskirts of town. Dinner only, closed Sundays.

### Mandri   ‖‖‖

*27 Arch. Kyprianos Ave., Strovolos. Tel. 49 72 00*

First-class traditional *meze*, copious set menu, friendly service in a large house in south-west suburb. Dinner only.

### Plaka  ▌▌
*8 Arch. Makarios Sq,*
*Engomi. Tel. 44 64 98*
Good Cypriot food, generous portions, in big boisterous tavern west of city centre, popular with Nicosians. Dinner only, closed Sundays.

## LIMASSOL/ GERMASOGEIA

### Anotera  ▌▌
*1 Gladstone St. Tel. 35 40 33*
Good *meze* (32 dishes!), grills and fresh fish à la carte in agreeable house near the New Post Office.

### Edo Lemesos  ▌▌▌
*Irini St. Tel. 36 79 81*
Excellent, copious *meze* menu served in lively taverna, first-class live music entertainment. Dinner only, closed Sundays.

### Farm House (Agrotospito)  ▌▌
*1 Ayios Paraskevis,*
*Germasogeia. Tel. 32 32 10*
Traditional Cypriot *meze* and fresh fish served in old-fashioned village style.

### Flogiera  ▌▌
*25 Patron St, Germasogeia.*
*Tel. 32 57 51*
Fine traditional food in old-fashioned rustic setting, friendly service, guitar music in evenings. Closed Sundays.

## LARNACA

### Massis  ▌▌
*Mackenzie Beach.*
*Tel. 65 60 22*
Good opportunity to compare Lebanese and Cypriot dishes, fresh fish, in seafront restaurant south of city centre.

### Militzis  ▌▌
*42 Piale Pasha St.*
*Tel. 65 58 67*
Generous *meze* or à la carte traditional food. Just south of old Turkish fort.

### Romantzo  ▌
*Larnaca–Dhekelia Rd.*
*Tel. 72 17 88*
Fish tavern well situated out on Larnaca Bay east of city centre. Bouzouki music, 'Cyprus night' Wednesdays.

**71**

# PAPHOS & Region

### Akamas
*Grivas Dighenis St, Polis. Tel. 32 15 20*
Convenient for visitors to Baths of Aphrodite or ramblers on Akamas Peninsula, taverna serving traditional food.

### Demokritos
*1 Dionyssou St, Kato Paphos. Tel. 23 33 71*
Just behind the port, lively, friendly taverna serving good *meze* and à la carte meals with live music entertainment.

### Latchi Fish Tavern
*Latchi harbour. Tel. 32 14 11*
Portside fish restaurant, catch of the day right from Chrysochou Bay.

### Tsiakkas
*Kissonerga (nr. Cynthiana Hotel). Tel. 24 34 59*
On road to Coral Bay, beachfront restaurant serving moussaka, kleftiko, local specialities and fresh fish.

# AYIA NAPA & Region

### Limnara
*Cape Greco St. Tel. 72 11 61*
Kleftiko, stifado and other Cypriot specialities.

### Savvides Kalamaras
*Protaras. Tel. 83 12 93*
Fresh fish, Greek cuisine and *meze*.

# TROODOS MOUNTAINS

### Mandra Gardens
*Pano Platres Tel. (05) 42 18 88*
Traditional Cypriot dishes, *meze* and live music.

### Psilon Dhendron
*Platres–Limassol Road. Tel. (05) 42 13 50*
The trout farm cooks your fresh trout any way you like it.

### Maryland & The Mill
*Kakopetria river. Tel. (02) 92 25 36, 92 29 29*
Fresh trout *au bleu* or grilled, traditional *souvla* and *kleftiko*.

# Paphos

Paphos has been transformed by the tourist boom that has concentrated in the southern part of the island since the 1974 partition. Resort facilities have expanded at a lightning rate, north to the beaches of Coral Bay and south from the old harbour out along Poseidon Avenue to Moulia. But visitors who want to do more than just lie in the sun have plenty to occupy them. Paphos is a comfortable base from which to explore the western mountain villages and monasteries and the beautiful nature trails on the Akamas peninsula, not forgetting the ancient sites of Paphos' long history back to when Aphrodite first made it her home.

Legend attributes the founding of Palea (Old) Paphos to the priest-king Cinyras. A temple was built to Aphrodite here, 16 km (10 miles) from today's Paphos, in Mycenaen times, and the city-kingdom gained renown as the centre of Aphrodite's cult. Earthquakes destroyed the temple sometime in the late 12th century BC, but it was rebuilt soon after by King Agapenor from Arcadia in the Peloponnese, who was shipwrecked in the area on his return from the Trojan War. Agapenor subsequently set himself up as king of Paphos.

The last king of Old Paphos, Nicocles, established the new port town of Nea Paphos late in the 4th century BC, though Palea Paphos remained the centre of Aphrodite worship until the 4th century AD. Within 100 years of its founding, Nea Paphos surpassed Salamis as chief city of Cyprus and it was here that, when Cyprus came under Roman government, the Proconsul Sergius Paulus was converted to Christianity. Earthquakes in 332 and 342 and Saracen attacks in the 7th century forced most of the population inland to Ktima, though Nea Paphos was not completely abandoned until 1372, following the Genoese invasion.

A small seaport for crusaders and others, Paphos languished as a miserable place **73** with a poor reputation. However, the population gradually increased to over 2,000 by the late 19th century. The harbour was dredged in 1908, attracting further maritime commerce. Paphos continued to grow and prosper, and in spite of some damage in the 1974 war, it bounced back to attract not only tourists but new Cypriot settlers also.

## KATO (LOWER) PAPHOS

West of the seafront restaurants and boutiques, the **harbour** still provides a haven for a few fishing boats and sailing vessels as it curves around a jetty to the old **Fort**. Like a child's building-blocks, virtually the same masonry has over the centuries been set up, knocked down and rearranged to form a Roman fort, a feudal castle, a Turkish tower and a British warehouse for salt.

From the east end of the harbour, Apostolos Pavlos Avenue climbs to the excavated site of an **Early Christian basilica** (4th century AD).

Among the ruins of the large seven-aisled church, you can make out mosaic pavements with floral and geometric patterns, Corinthian capitals and columns of green and white marble imported from Greece. Arabic graffiti on some of the columns date from the invasion which destroyed the basilica in AD 653. One of the columns is still described as **St Paul's Pillar** where the apostle was imagined to have been tied and lashed 39 times for preaching the Gospel – more than 300 years before the marble reached Cyprus.

Still standing intact is the 15th-century **Ayia Kyriaki church** at which Catholic and Anglican services are held. Nearby are the vestiges of a Gothic Franciscan church put up by the Lusignans. But note, too, just to the north of the Christian sanctuaries, a tiny twin-domed secular building,

*Take a boat from the old port of Paphos and explore the romantic coastline.*

**74**

the old **Turkish baths**, with a gnarled old tree trunk pushing up through the masonry.

West of Apostolos Pavlos Avenue lies the so-called **Byzantine Castle**, also popularly known as *Saranda Kolones* – 40 columns – after the number of granite columns found lying around here. Excavations have since established its true identity as a castle built by French Crusaders at the end of the 12th century and destroyed by earthquake in 1222. Its large square keep had a tower at each corner, surrounded by a dry moat and thick exterior walls with eight bastions.

On your way to the nearby Roman remains, make a short detour north to the **Odeon**, a reconstructed amphitheatre of the 2nd century AD. In a picturesque hillside setting with a lighthouse behind it, it seats 1,250 spectators for open-air shows.

## THE PAPHOS MOSAICS

The splendid decorative floors that have been (and are still being) uncovered in the re-

mains of wealthy Roman villas of Nea (New) Paphos (3rd century AD) constitute the most important group of mosaics in Cyprus. Lovingly reconstructed from damage suffered during the land-levelling operations which first revealed them in 1962 and the bombardments in 1974, they are exhibited in houses named after the mosaics' most prominent motif. The *tesserae* (mosaic cubes) are bright coloured local stone of natural hues, together with some orange, yellow, green and blue glass.

The **House of Dionysos** displays the god of wine returning from India on a chariot drawn by two panthers. This and other scenes, such as Dionysos recommending moderation to the nymph Akme drinking wine from a bowl, and King Icarios of Athens getting shepherds drunk with their first taste of wine, were customary decorations for the dining room. But here are also romantic scenes of Pyramos and Thisbe and of Phaedra looking longingly at her stepson Hippolytos. More

dramatic are the hunting motifs of leopard, tiger and bear around the atrium.

Follow the signposts to the **Villa of Theseus**, probably the official residence of the Proconsul of Nea Paphos, where the mosaic shows Ariadne watching a heroic but rather absent-minded Theseus slay the (partially defaced) Minotaur. The **House of Aion** has a spectacular five-panelled mosaic. The large central panel depicts Aion, god of eternity, judging a beauty contest between a somewhat smug-looking Queen Cassiopeia, the winner, and the unhappy, unquestionably prettier Nereides water nymphs.

## TOMBS OF THE KINGS

North-west of what was Nea Paphos (off the road to the beach resort of **Coral Bay**) is the ancient community's necropolis. Its subterranean burial chambers were carved from the ruddy rock that slopes down to the sea at a time (3rd century BC to 3rd century AD) when Paphos had

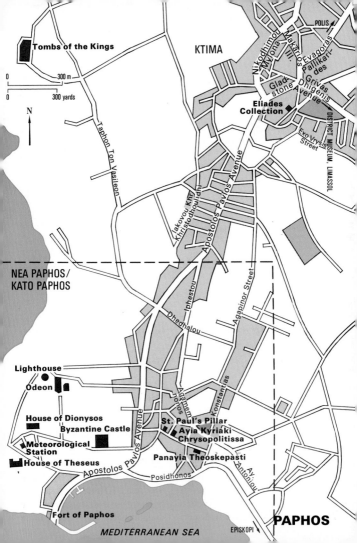

**Tombs of the Kings**

KTIMA

POLIS

Nikodhimou
Mylona
Makarios III.
Evagoras Pallikari-
des
Grivas
Glad-
stone Avenue
Dhigenis

0     300 m
0     300 yards

N

DISTRICT MUSEUM, LIMASSOL

**Eliades
Collection**

Exo Vrysis
Street

Taphon Ton Vasileon

Iakovou Kml
Khristodhoulidhi
Apostolos Pavlos Avenue

NEA PAPHOS/
KATO PAPHOS

Iphestou

Agapinor Street

Dhedhalou

**Lighthouse**

**Odeon**

**House of Dionysos**

**Byzantine Castle**

**Meteorological
Station**

**House of Theseus**

Pavlos Avenue

Agamemnonos

Konstantias

**St. Paul's Pillar**

**Ayia Kyriaki
Chrysopolitissa**

**Panayia Theoskepasti**

Ayiou
Antoniou

Apostolos Pavlos Avenue

Posidhonos

**Fort of Paphos**

MEDITERRANEAN SEA

EPISKOPI

**PAPHOS**

*The ancient Tombs of the Kings served as refuge for Christians during early persecutions.*

no kings. But many of them are imposing enough to suggest that they were at least the resting place of the Ptolemy dynasty's most important local officials. This 'city of the dead', imitating in those days the city of the living, gives a rare insight into the residential architecture of Nea Paphos: spacious courtyards with peri-

style of Doric columns and decorative entablatures.

## THE UPPER TOWN

Away from the resort cafés and hotels on a beautiful hilltop site 42 m (140 ft) above the sea, **Ktima** is a bright, modern area distinguished by Neoclassical school and bank

**78**

buildings, green open spaces and a large market.

On the road to Limassol (Dighenis Avenue) is the small **Paphos District Museum**. It houses some remarkable sculptures found in the Roman 'Villa of Theseus'. Carved in white marble imported from the Aegean, they include fine statues of Aphrodite, Dionysos, the divine huntress Artemis (also known as Diana) and Asclepios, Greek master of medicine, feeding an egg to the snake coiled around his staff. Notice, too, the Egyptian goddess Isis, an exquisite head with heavy-lidded eyes. There are also fine collections of jewellery, coins, ceramics and ancient glassware.

A more modest museum, but also worth a visit, is housed in a charming 19th century house, the **Eliades Collection**, Exo Vrysis Street near the Bishop's Palace. It combines prehistoric fossils, classical antiquities and Cypriot folklore of the 18th and 19th centuries. In the garden, Professor George Eliades has

uncovered, carved in the bedrock, burial chambers from the 3rd century BC.

## EAST OF PAPHOS

Just east of town on the road to Paphos Airport is the village of **Yeroskipos**. Its name means 'Sacred Garden'. Dedicated to Aphrodite, pilgrims from Nea Paphos stopped off on their way to the goddess's temple at Palea Paphos; today, Turkish delight is manufactured here.

The 11th-century church of **Ayia Paraskevi** is, for Cyprus, a rare example of a five-domed basilica. Inside are some 15th-century murals and a much revered icon, also 15th century, with a *Virgin and Child* on one side and *Crucifixion* on the reverse.

In a restored house nearby is the **Museum of Folk Art**. Typical of an 18th-century rich Cypriot's villa, it has an upper storey surrounded with handsome wooden balconies. The house once belonged to Andreas Zimboulakis, British consular agent for Paphos – a **79**

## The Love Goddess

What the ancients seemed to like about Aphrodite was that she enjoyed her work. A lot of the other goddesses wanted to borrow her magic girdle, which made every male fall in love with its wearer, but she just would not part with it.

She found her husband Hephaestos, the gods' blacksmith, a bit too sweaty, and terribly gullible. She had three children with her lover Ares, god of war, without poor Hephaestos guessing until Helios the Sun gossiped about what he had seen when rising one morning. Hephaestos promptly fashioned a gossamer-thin but unsnappable bronze net with which he trapped Aphrodite in bed with Ares the next night.

Unperturbed at the ensuing divorce trial, Aphrodite only had eyes for the flighty trickster Hermes, who was muttering that he would not have minded being under that net with her. He soon had his wish and the result was the double-sexed Hermaphrodite.

Making love was the only job the Fates had given her One day, she was found using a loom and Athene was furious at this breach of her prerogative. Aphrodite graciously apologized and was never again found doing anything but making love.

post Andreas and then his son held from 1799 to 1865. Museum displays include gourds that kept children afloat while they learned to swim, even jars of carob honey, from which you can take a taste. You will also see agricultural tools, elaborately carved furniture, a lovely 18th-century painted grandfather clock, and other items.

From Yeroskipos, continue east about 12 km (8 miles) and turn off at **Kouklia**, once Palea Paphos, where the cult of Aphrodite took place. The love-goddess rites flourished at the **Sanctuary of Aphrodite** from very early times. Homer described the yearly spring festival – the Mysteries – which contributed much to the fame and coffers of

Cyprus, as pilgrims came from all over the ancient world. Now in the Cyprus Museum in Nicosia, a conical stone symbolizing the goddess (her beauty was too great to represent literally) was the symbolic centre of Aphrodite worship.

Alas, little remains of romance in the ruins on view in Kouklia, a small farming community. Aphrodite seems to have wafted away on a zephyr, the way she came. Archaeologists have been at work here since the late 19th century, uncovering the sanctuary – believed to lie largely under some surrounding farm dwellings. You can distinguish north and south stoas or halls, and some cyclopean blocks of a Bronze Age wall.

The Château de Covocle nearby – originally a Lusignan fort, and then a Turkish manor house and farm – contains the collection of the **Palea Paphos Museum**. Although many of the valuable finds from the sanctuary have been taken to Nicosia (such as a mosaic of *Leda and the Swan*, once stolen from here and later recovered), there are still some ceramics and other objects of minor interest.

## NORTH OF PAPHOS

Leaving the coast road to the resort hotels on your left, take the other north-bound highway (signposted **Polis**) inland. Just 10 km (6 miles) north of Paphos the **Monastery of Ayios Neophytos** dominates a peaceful, wooded slope. Its church has some good 15th- and 16th-century frescoes and icons, but the main focus, set in the hill-side opposite the church, is the 12th-century **Englistra** (Hermitage), around which the monastery grew up. The saintly historian and theologian Neophytos (1134–1214) hacked this cave-dwelling out of the rock with his own hands. He supervised the wonderful frescoes which decorate the chapel, sanctuary and cell. One scene shows Neophytos himself, flanked by the archangels Michael and Gabriel.

On the north coast, the town of **Polis** stands where the **81**

ancient city-kingdom of Marion boasted rich gold and copper mines. The modern town is a gateway to the pleasant sponge-fishing port and beach resort of **Latchi** with good facilities for water sports.

Romantics should head a little way down the road to the **Baths of Aphrodite** *(Loutra tis Aphroditis)*, a natural pool and springs set in a cool green glade where our local heroine bathed to rejuvenate herself.

The **Akamas Peninsula** is a superb nature reserve, one of the few unspoiled wildernesses left on the island (but occasionally off-limits if the British army is using part of it for shooting practice!). Nature trails are marked out along the craggy north shore. One of them leads ostensibly to **Fontana Amorosa**, in fact just a muddy well, but the ramble itself is worth while. Make your way among scrub forest of pine and juniper and stunted olive and carob trees leading over to dramatic cliffs of dark volcanic rock.

A peculiarity of the peninsula is the *Arbutus* (strawberry tree), with bright green foliage and fruit that look like (but taste nothing like) strawberries. Wild flowers include the bright red Cyprus tulip, pink or yellow anemone and many varieties of orchid. Birdwatchers can spot the black francolin, bright blue roller and the migrant bee eater or crested hoopoe, while butterfly buffs may see the rare two-tailed pasha or the commoner orange and yellow cleopatra.

While the monastery of Panayia Chrysorroyiatissa may be reached via some rather perilous mountain roads from Troodos, it is much easier to make the excursion from Paphos. Again take the road north to Polis, turning to **Polemi** and continuing on through **Pano Panayia**, the birthplace in 1913 of Mihail Mouskos, who became the archbishop and later president, Makarios III.

*T*he Baths of Aphrodite, where the goddess supposedly met her young suitors.

**Panayia Chrysorroyiatissa** ('Our Lady of the Golden Pomegranate') perches on a hilly site with orchards and vineyards around it. Vines have been there since the 12th century, but only recently the monastery has started producing wines again, one of them a prize-winning white. The monk Ignatios founded the monastery in 1152; the present complex dates from the late 18th century, and was restored in 1955. The cloister is built on an unusual triangular plan. Within the enclosure stands the church, noted for its elaborately carved iconostasis. A heavy silver-gilt case encloses the chief icon of the Virgin, framed in silver, a favourite of criminals and outlaws seeking divine help.

# Northern Cyprus

The frustration for Greek Cypriots is not just that the Turkish-occupied north (37 % of the island) is forbidden territory, but that it is a most beautiful region. The Kyrenia Mountains have a gaunt unspoiled splendour, the ports of Famagusta and Kyrenia have not lost the romance of their past, nor have ancient Salamis or the Gothic crusader castles and Bellapais abbey. In two day trips you can see all the sights comfortably, including northern Nicosia (see p. 38).

## THE MOUNTAIN CASTLES

Most striking of the Kyrenia mountains rising beyond Nicosia is the Pentadaktylos (Five Fingers) whose stark silhouette gives the range its second name. In *Bitter Lemons*, Lawrence Durrell, who lived on their northern slopes, calls the chain '*par excellence* the Gothic range, for it is studded with crusader castles pitched on the dizzy spines of the mountains, commanding the roads which run over the saddles between.'

These Gothic fortresses lie now in noble ruin, victim not of enemy bombardment but of dismantlement by the Venetians who could not afford their upkeep, the weather doing the rest. Most spectacular is **St Hilarion Castle**, climbing in three tiers of battlements and towers up to a 670-m (2,200-ft) mountain peak. (Be prepared for some uphill walking to tackle all three levels.) The castle was built around a church and monastery of the 10th century honouring the hermit-saint Hilarion, who fled here when the Arabs advanced on Syria. An original Byzantine structure was fortified and extended by the Lusignans for their summer residence.

Standing against formidable winds, as its name suggests, **Buffavento**, is the highest of the castles – 954 m (3,129 ft). It is little more now than a pile of crumbling stone – accessible by car or donkey – but once proudly defended the shortest approach from the coast to Nicosia.

Farthest east, **Kantara Castle** was built by the Byzantines to control the Karpas peninsula after the departure of the Arabs in 965. The ruin offers from its uppermost

tower, 630 m (2,068 ft), an exquisite view of woodland and olive groves along the north coast. It was from here that the guard sent out flare signals to Buffavento which relayed them to St Hilarion, Kyrenia and Nicosia.

## KYRENIA

With sheltered harbour and a grand old castle, this charming town – *Girne* in Turkish – is the best place to stop for lunch. It has a genuine resort atmosphere, more relaxed than its sisters on the south coast.

The massive **Castle** was used as a prison by each of the island's rulers from the Byzantines to the British, the latter locking up EOKA fighters here in the 1950s. The walls enclose a Byzantine chapel, royal apartments, and the tomb of Turkish admiral Sadik Pasha, conqueror of Kyrenia in 1570. Not least, it serves as a museum for the **Kyrenia Ship**, one of the oldest vessels ever recovered from the sea. This Greek trading ship sank off the coast here

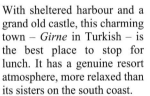

about 300 BC and was discovered in 1965 by a sponge diver. The hull has been painstakingly reconstructed and is shown with part of its cargo – Rhodian wine jars, millstones, cooking utensils and a consignment of almonds.

## BELLAPAIS ABBEY

A short drive into the foothills behind Kyrenia leads to this superbly situated 13th- and 14th-century Gothic abbey. Looking down to the distant sea, it stands on a 30-m (100-ft) escarpment, its monastery buildings enclosing cypress trees, palms, orange and olive trees. Though 'beautiful country' would be an entirely appropriate explanation for its name, it was more probably Abbey of Peace *(Abbaye de la Paix)*, built by the Lusignans for the Augustinian order. The elegant arcade of the **cloister** is adorned with finely carved figures: a fox, an ass, a hero fighting two monsters. The vaulted **refectory** is a splendid space of six bays with a well-preserved rose window.

Among vestiges of the monks' wooden benches, the one on the east wall is set higher, probably for the Abbot's High Table.

The surrounding village was Lawrence Durrell's *Bitter Lemons* home, but friends and their families have all sought refuge elsewhere and their Tree of Idleness has died.

## FAMAGUSTA

On the island's east coast, the port was only a village when Christian refugees arrived in 1291 from Palestine. A century later, it was a notorious boom town of extravagant merchants, courtesans and colourful rascals. That all ended in 1571 when the Turks massacred its citizens after a prolonged siege (see p. 20).

It rose again to become in this century the most important port in Cyprus and a major tourist centre. But the invasion of 1974, less bloodthirsty but still traumatic, left Famagusta – *Gazimagusa* in Turkish – only a shadow of its former self. Since the departure of

### Visiting the North

The only way across the Attila Line is through Nicosia beside the old Ledra Palace Hotel on Marcos Drakos Avenue. The border crossing opens up about 8 a.m. Be there early to get in a full day's tour before nightfall – obligatory time of return may vary from 4.30 to 6 p.m. Before crossing, with passport, you must check in with the Greek-Cypriot duty officer. You cannot drive over, but Turkish-Cypriot taxis – individual or shared service – are waiting on the other side. At the Turkish control point, you buy a visa for one Greek-Cypriot pound. You can change money into Turkish-Cypriot lira for museums and meals, but Greek-Cypriot money is accepted. You can take photographs, but only of non-military or non-sensitive subjects, on which your Turkish-Cypriot taxi driver will advise you. He will know if some places we describe are off-limits – when the Turkish army is training.

**87**

Greek Cypriots from the southern part of town, Varosha, the beach resort area is deserted and off-limits. Yet the Venetian fortifications and old town where the Turkish Cypriots always traditionally lived are still of great interest.

Down by the harbour stands the Citadel, better known as the **Tower of Othello**, associated with a 16th-century Lieutenant-Governor of Cyprus named Christoforo Moro, who was possibly the model for Shakespeare's tormented Moor. Notice the crest of Venice's winged lion of St Mark over the barrel-arched entry. The moated tower has four corner turrets and a good view over the port – one of those places where photography is risky.

Most formidable of the Venetian fortifications is the **Martinengo Bastion** in the north-west corner of the old town. In the siege, the Turks inspected its walls, 4–6 m (13–19 ft) thick, and looked for something easier.

The Lusignans built the town's churches, at one time numbering 365. The finest of these was **St Nicholas Cathedral**, converted with one slim minaret to become the Lala Mustafa Pasha Mosque (named after the commander of the Turkish invasion of 1570). The fine French Gothic structure was completed in 1326 with a majestic western façade worthy of any of the great cathedrals 'back home'. Although as a mosque the interior has been stripped of human representation in sculpture or fresco – and damaged by earthquake in 1735 – it can be admired for its pristine Gothic features, uncluttered by the Baroque or Neo-Gothic additions it might have suffered elsewhere.

Nearby is the elegant **Venetian Governor's Palace** *(Palazzo del Provveditore)*. The three noble arches adorning its Renaissance façade stand on four Doric columns brought from the ancient site of Salamis. Later, as a prison, the palace entertained the 19th-century Turkish national poet Namik Kemal for three years for criticizing the Sultan.

## SALAMIS

Directly overlooking the sea just 9 km (5 miles) north of Famagusta, this ancient city-kingdom ranks with Kourion as the finest archaeological site on the island. For 2,000 years, Salamis was the leading power in Cyprus, counting 100,000 citizens at its height, a huge population for the time. It was a favourite haven for Greek artists and intellectuals exiled from Athens. As Constantia, it became capital of early Christian Cyprus in AD 395, subsequently declining from earthquake destruction and disappearing completely after the Arab invasion of 647.

Visible ruins today date from Hellenistic, Roman and Byzantine times. The Roman **Theatre** (2nd century AD) probably succeeded an earlier Greek structure. The 50-row auditorium seated 15,000, the largest in Cyprus. Most impressive is the spacious **Gymnasium** (high school). The graceful Corinthian columns were brought here from the Theatre and re-erected by the Byzantines. In the adjoining **Public Baths**, you can distinguish the *frigidarium, tepidarium* and the hot room – *caldarium* – with water heated by furnaces beneath the floor. The water itself was channelled from Kythrea, 60 km (37 miles) away via a Roman aqueduct still standing.

## ST BARNABAS MONASTERY

A couple of minutes' drive west of Salamis is the mausoleum of Barnabas, fellow apostle of Paul on their mission to Cyprus in AD 45. (He achieved martyrdom in Salamis at the hands of Jews he was trying to convert.) The rock-cut burial chamber is now empty, but its discovery some 400 years later helped the Church of Cyprus achieve autonomy within the Orthodox faith (see p. 16) and led to the building of the monastery nearby. The present drum-domed church was built in 1756 with elements from an earlier 15th-century church and columns and capitals from Salamis.

**89**

# What to Do

Cyprus is an active, lively place where there is plenty to do beyond sightseeing. Shopping can take in traditional craftware, fine jewellery and copies of ancient artwork. And you may encounter the additional pleasure of 'negotiating' a fair price with the friendliest, least aggressive merchants in the Mediterranean – which does not mean they make no profit. Sporting activities benefit from a great climate and amazingly clear coastal waters. Entertainment can offer anything from bouzouki to hot rock, with plenty of folklore at the village festivals and even a play or concert in the grand setting of an ancient open-air theatre.

## Sports

The miracle of Cyprus's beaches is their unpolluted sea. For water-sports enthusiasts in the Mediterranean these days that is no mean achievement. Ramblers find their joy in the unspoiled mountain country of the interior or along the rugged coastline at the north-west tip of the island.

### WATER SPORTS

The facilities for **swimming** vary from the sandy family beaches of Coral Bay north of Paphos and at Ayia Napa

and Protaras to more secluded cove-bathing in Chrysochou Bay along the Akamas Peninsula or out at the island's opposite, south-east, tip around Cape Greco. For a pagan tryst, try Aphrodite's birthplace at Petra tou Romiou.

In all the major resorts, the Cyprus Tourist Organization sponsors excellent public beaches, most often sandy,

*Paragliding is just one of the many water sports that can be enjoyed in Ayia Napa.*

beautifully laid out with grass around them. Amenities include changing rooms, bar-restaurants and courts for basket- and volleyball.

The bigger hotels have excellent freshwater pools, some Olympic size. Most admit non-residents for a fee.

**Scuba-diving** and **snorkelling** lovers are the major beneficiaries of Cyprus's limpid seas, perfect for underwater photography. In water temperatures varying from 16°C (60°F) to 27°C (80°F) you can explore submerged cliffs, valleys and colonies of coral, and get close-up views of sea anemones and sponges, exotic coloured fish and crustacea. Remember that it is a criminal offence to remove antiquities from the seabed, but by all means report sightings to the local archaeological museum.

You will find diving centres with rental equipment and instruction at Paphos, Coral Bay, Lachi (near Polis), Larnaca, Limassol, Ayia Napa and Paralimni.

**Windsurfing** and **waterskiing** are available everywhere, with equipment for hire at public and hotel beaches. The adventurous like **parasailing**, the well-heeled can hire a yacht for **sailing**, but hiring a **canoe** or **pedalo** is not expensive.

**Fishing** at sea, including spear-fishing, requires no licence and boats with or without captain are available for hire at most ports; the smaller ones are better, like Zygi, midway between Larnaca and Limassol, or Pomos, north of Polis. Local fishermen go for red mullet, white bream and amberjack. Dams at Asprokremmos east of Paphos and Germasogeia north of Limassol are stocked with trout, carp and other fresh-water fish, for which angling is permitted with a licence from the town's Fisheries Department. Enquire at the nearest tourist office.

## OTHER SPORTS

**Tennis.** Better hotels provide tennis courts (clay or asphalt) for guests, often available to non-residents for a fee. There are several courts at Nicosia's Field Club and at the Lapatsa Sporting Centre in Tseri (15 minutes from Nicosia).

**Horse Riding**. With an indoor arena and outdoor

**92**

paddock, the Lapatsa Sporting Centre offers a full equitation programme, from dressage and show jumping to cross-country riding (courses for beginners to advanced). In a totally different category, children or others can ride a horse or pony (for hire by the half-hour – usually at weekends) to sightsee around Troodos.

**Cycling**. Most towns and resorts have at least one shop where you can rent bicycles, with mountain bikes to tackle the Troodos and Paphos high country.

**Walking and Hiking**. You can trek through the Troodos chain and foothills, past pleasant mountain streams, many delightful villages and view-

*No holiday in Cyprus would be complete without at least one outing on the water.*

points. The Cyprus Tourism Organization distributes maps and information on itineraries. Tours are organized from abroad for excursions in the area from a base in Pano Platres or Troodos and along the Akamas Peninsula.

## WINTER SPORTS

Promoters of the Troodos mountains resort area would like to see more people take advantage of winter as a time to visit Cyprus, when lower prices are in force. Lifts provide access to several runs on Mount Olympus, and more are being developed. Cross-country skiing is also possible. Depending on snow conditions, the ski season runs from January to early March.

## SPECTATOR SPORTS

**Car Racing**. A big event in European racing, the 72-hour

*Riding in tandem on the beach at Paphos.*

international Cyprus Rally in September attracts up to 80 entrants for a gruelling trial of endurance, guts and skill. Check the local newspapers for details of the route.

**Horse Racing**. Race meetings take place once or twice a week from mid-September to the end of June (Saturdays or Sundays) at the Nicosia Racecourse in Ayios Dhometios.

# Shopping

The efficiency of modern international trade has made the same range of consumer products available all over the world – electronic gadgetry, leisure-wear and sports equipment are no cheaper here than elsewhere. So stick to the high-quality products of the island's traditional artisans.

Most shops open from 8 a.m. to 1 p.m., take a leisurely lunch-cum-siesta and re-open from 4 to 7 p.m. Blame afternoon closing on Wednesdays on the British Empire and on Saturdays on local initiative.

## BEST BUYS

Rural arts and crafts have been given a big boost in recent years with the influx of Greek-Cypriot refugees from the north. They are the principal artisans at shops run by the Cyprus Handicraft Service (CHS), a non-profit organization with outlets in Nicosia, Limassol, Larnaca and Paphos.

**Basketry.** The choice ranges from small baskets in decorative shapes and colours to large articles in rush or cane.

**Brass.** Look for candlesticks, ashtrays, small boxes, religious ornaments and trays.

**Carpets and curtains.** In Cypriot patterns, with a Near-Eastern and Turkish influence, these can be colourful and in good taste. The woollen rugs in all sizes are very tempting.

**Ceramics.** Many artisans look back to antiquity for inspiration, creating charming animal figurines, little vessels and terracotta statuettes, fashioned by hand and fired. The functional wares of Kornos and Phini include attractive hand-thrown wine and oil jars. **95**

*This 'lace'-maker's house in Kato Lefkara is a treasure trove for the dedicated souvenir hunter.*

Glazed ceramics may have very pretty geometric patterns in the Cypriot style.

**Copperware.** Dating from over 3,000 years ago, the copper industry remains a source of Cypriot pride. There are all manner of hand-crafted ware, including copper pots, saucepans and bowls.

**Embroidery.** Shops all over Cyprus sell the island's most important cottage indus-

try item – fine linen table-cloths, doilies, runners and handkerchiefs stitched with intricate geometic patterns of Lefkara (see p. 48).

**Food and wine.** Turkish Delight *(loukhoumi)* is a speciality of Yeroskipos and Lefkara – though shops all over sell it. You may want to carry home Cypriot olives or sealed packets of the local cheese, *halloumi*. Of the many wines and liqueurs produced on Cyprus, you might purchase some Commandaria, the sweet red dessert wine.

**Jewellery.** You can find good quality silver and goldware, the latter almost always 18-karat (as opposed to Greece's more customary 14-karat gold). Reputable jewellers will always provide a certificate of authenticity if requested.

**Leather goods.** Manufactured locally, shoes and sandals are reasonably priced and well-styled on Cyprus, especially models for women. Appealing presents for yourself and others include hand-tooled handbags, belts and wallets – as well as soft leather jackets, waistcoats (vests), skirts and trousers.

**Souvenirs.** Gifts with a local touch range from colourful Cypriot stamps and stamp gift booklets (at larger post offices), coins and maps, to records and cassettes of Cypriot music.

**Wooden articles.** Craftsmen produce everything from elaborate picture-frames to traditional Cypriot-style dowry chests. At the Nicosia outlet of the Cyprus Handicrafts Service you can order custom-made furniture, to be shipped home.

**Woollen goods.** Heavy patterned sweaters, tie belts and shawls have a rustic appeal. Woollen shoulder bags are another speciality.

**Woven goods.** Colourful, hand-loomed fabrics made up into dresses, children's clothing and shirts for men and women at reasonable prices.

# Entertainment

Bars and restaurants catering specifically for tourists provide music, both traditional *bouzouki* and international pop, rock and disco, late into the night in all the resorts, particularly around the harbour. Strolling musicians occasionally liven up the night scene at quaysides and in the tavernas.

If you want to find where the young Cypriots go, follow their motor scooters down the **97** back streets behind the ports of Limassol, Larnaca and Paphos. Nicosia's tavernas are more traditional. But Limassol's cabarets provide the liveliest night out, keeping the Arab and Lebanese colony entertained until the small hours.

Most hotels offer weekly folklore shows with Cypriot-costumed performers singing and dancing to charming village tunes. Visitors are invariably encouraged to get up and dance along – and nobody objects to missteps. Hotels also organize special buffets and cocktail parties, gaming nights and fashion shows.

The Nicosia Municipal Theatre stages plays in Greek and sometimes English; concerts are held here, too. Films in English are shown in the larger cities. Ask at your hotel or consult local papers and *Cyprus Time Out* for information about special events.

A Cyprus-by-night tour might take you to a local restaurant to sample *mezedes* and on to a performance of traditional Cypriot dancing with *bouzouki* music. Some tours include a pastiche of a Cypriot wedding full in swing.

## FESTIVALS AND HOLY DAYS

Listed below are just a few of the principal events, as every town commemorates its patron saint, from Luke to Neophytos. Feast days and other holidays bring out the inevitable merchants and their stands *(paniyiri)* of market produce, sweets, drinks and trinkets.

**January**

*Ta Fota*. On Epiphany Day (6 January), bishops bless the waters in all the seaside towns, throwing their Holy Crosses into the sea. Boys dive for them, winning a small prize when they surface with one.

**February/March**

*Clean Monday*. Large amounts of vegetables, olives and wine are consumed on this day of 'fasting', the Monday before Lent.

*Carnival*. Limassol's ten-day long celebration features fancy-dress balls and a spate of parades. It's not Rio, but it's light-hearted.

## March/April

*Good Friday*. Orthodox Solemn Masses take place all over Cyprus, with a procession of the Holy Sepulchre in main streets and squares.

*Easter*. A midnight service takes place on the Saturday before Easter, when people light their candles from the priest's, moving around the church and chanting the litany in a kind of sound-and-light atmosphere that is nevertheless fervently religious. On Easter Sunday, High Masses celebrate the resurrection of Christ. The rest of the day is devoted to socializing, eating and games.

## May/June

*Kataklismos*. Also known as Pentecost, this two-day holiday harks back to ancient times, when Cypriots convened at temples to worship and sacrifice to Adonis and Aphrodite, continuing their celebrations down at the seashore. Nowadays there are excursions to the beach, parties, games, colourful parades, competitions and 'dousing' – especially at Paphos.

## August

*Assumption of the Virgin*. On 15 August, the faithful gather at the leading monasteries: Kykko, Chrysorroyiatissa, Troodhitissa, Macheras. (Beware of crowds: the small roads leading to the churches can be clogged with cars.)

*Lefkara Festival*. In mid-August, Lefkara holds a village festival to display its famous embroidery and other crafts. There's music, dancing and food stands galore.

## September

*The Virgin Nativity*. On 8 September, a crowd assembles at Kykko Monastery to observe rites from icon-kissing to lemonade-drinking.

*Nicosia Arts Festival*. This two-week long event features everything from art exhibitions and folk dancing to avant-garde ballet and rock concerts. Most of the events take place in the Famagusta Gate Cultural Centre.

*Limassol Wine Festival*. A fortnight of wine-tastings, dancing and folklore shows.

*Ayia Napa Festival*. Folklore, music, dance and theatre. **99**

# Eating Out

People in Cyprus eat well and plenty; they are not a thin race. Their island has the cuisine of its geography and history – conquerors and refugees alike have left their mark – Turkish, Greek, Syrian, Lebanese and Armenian. And the modern Republic has the prosperity to make the combination distinctive: good fresh vegetables, tangy meat dishes, fish and seafood – savoury but undisguised by dubious sauces. Best of all is that mind-boggling procession of *mezedes* where you have the delightful problem the French call *embarras du choix* – too much to choose from.

But with mass tourism has come that bland hybrid called 'international cuisine' getting in the way of the real local food. And British-style fish-and-chips is being overtaken by the ubiquitous hamburger and pizza. But take heart: such local fast-food items as pitta bread with *sheftalia* (a kind of sausage) and *souvlaki* (skewered meat) are not yet mass-produced and the quality can be high.

As opposed to Greece, where you're encouraged to rush in to the kitchen to point out what you'd like to eat, Cyprus restaurants usually expect you to order from the menu (almost invariably translated into English and perhaps other languages), with the waiter's help. Some traditional Cypriot tavernas have no menu, just a set meal and you pay a fixed price for whatever is being served that night: trust them and enjoy your meal.

In Mediterranean fashion, local people tend to eat late (from 1.30 to 3.30 p.m. for lunch, 9 to 10.30 p.m. for dinner). But service begins an hour or even two hours earlier. Things are quieter, but you'll usually get good service if you come then – also a good idea if you're eating with young children. To be sure of eating in the company of Cypriots, come later.

As Cyprus produces excellent wine, beer and brandy, reasonably priced drinks

*R*elax over a drink in the glorious setting of Paphos harbour – and admire the view of the old fort.

before, during or after meals can contribute to the general euphoria.

## BREAKFAST

The usual hotel breakfast is continental: rolls, toast or bread, biscuits and perhaps croissants with butter and jam, and coffee, tea or chocolate. The tea will probably be made from tea bags, and the coffee is all too often hot water, provided with an envelope or two of instant powder, to be added to taste.

For big appetites, some hotels offer an English-style breakfast of ham and eggs, perhaps porridge or kippers. Some international hotel menus also list American-style breakfast cereals. Fresh fruits **101** and fruit juices are almost always available and they are delicious.

Those who prefer real coffee should order the 'Greek' or 'Turkish' variety, readily available at any time of day in cafés or tavernas. Order it sweet *(gliko)*, medium sweet *(metrio)*, or without sugar *(sketo)*. Greek coffee is taken black, never with cream or milk, and is usually accompanied by a glass of ice water.

## STARTERS

Hot and cold appetizers *(mezedes)* can be so varied and interesting that you could make a whole meal of them. Some restaurants offer menus of over 20 items. Naturally, in this food cornucopia, there is Greek-style *taramosalata* (fish-roe paste with oil, mashed potato or softened bread and lemon juice). *Dzadziki* (yoghurt with cucumber, crushed garlic and seasonings) is well known as a Greek or Turkish dish, but probably originated in Lebanon. *Talattouri*, a Cypriot variant of this preparation, will invariably be seasoned with fresh mint. Other popular dips include *tachinosalata* (sesame seed paste with garlic) and *hoummous*, a purée of chickpeas, olive oil and hot spices. To accompany these dips, you'll be served fresh Cypriot sesame seed *(koulouri)* bread, which has a hearty home-made taste, and may be toasted.

The array of *mezedes* continues with *melidzanosalata* (aubergine – eggplant – puréed with oil, garlic, a little vinegar, lemon juice and seasonings) and a small plate of black olives. You may be served a tomato salad, pickled capers and cauliflower *(moungra)* or spicy squid or octopus *(ktapodhi ksidhato)*, cut into small pieces.

Smoked sausages figure prominently among *mezedes* offerings, whether *sheftalia* (port, veal or lamb) or the ever-popular pork and beef *loukanika*. There is succulent marinated ham, pressed *(chiromeri)* or smoked *(lounza)*, and smoked fillet of pork, served hot (charcoal-grilled) or cold and thin-sliced. Do try *halloumi*, Cypriot ewe's milk cheese, which may be served hot (grilled or fried) or cold. *Dolmadakia* are the well-known vine leaves stuffed with rice, lamb and sometimes mint.

*Souvlakia*, skewered pieces of lamb (or chicken, beef or pork) grilled over charcoal, may be eaten as a starter or a main course – as may grilled lamb chops.

## SOUPS AND PASTA

Order hearty mixed vegetable, pea or lentil soup or the appealing *avgolemono*, a lemon-flavoured chicken broth thickened with egg and served with rice, of Greek origin. *Trachanas*, a healthy speciality, combines cracked wheat and yoghurt.

Fresh pasta – excellent and popular on Cyprus – may mean fettucini or tagliatelli with meat, cream or vegetable sauces. Be sure to try *kypriakes ravioles*, Cypriot ravioli stuffed with *halloumi* (ewe's milk cheese), eggs and mint.

## FISH AND SHELLFISH

Since offshore catches are relatively scanty, the choice of seafood may be limited. Shrimp, squid and spiny lobster appear on menus, but it's likely they will be frozen, rather than fresh. However, you may be offered fresh swordfish *(xifias)*, red mullet *(barbounia)*, red snapper *(sinagrida)* or a small Mediterranean fish called *psirika*. These varieties may be grilled, sautéed, stuffed and baked or, more rarely, cooked in a wine sauce. Some hotel chefs prepare salads of mixed shellfish (mussels, shrimp, spiny lobster), and they can be excellent. In the Troodos mountains the farm-raised trout are very good, whether smoked, sautéed, perhaps with slivered almonds, or *au bleu* (poached with clarified butter).

## MEAT AND VEGETABLES

Cypriots love the ubiquitous *moussaka* as much as Greeks do; this layered dish of minced meat, aubergine (eggplant) and marrows (squash), **103** potatoes, cream sauce and spices varies somewhat, according to the chef. A slightly different taste and texture characterize aubergine stuffed with minced meat and tomatoes and topped with beaten egg and breadcrumbs *(papoutsakia)*. *Stifado*, beef or veal stew, usually contains wine, onions and herb seasoning. *Patcha* is sheep's head stewed with lemon and garlic. Chicken *(kotopoulo)* may be barbecued, roasted, or served in a casserole with sauce, and perhaps mushrooms and onions as well.

A variety of plain grilled steaks and chops feature on all menus. Lamb is cooked in a kind of clay pot with vegetables and spices *(tavas)* or cut into chops and kebabs and barbecued *(kleftiko)*. Pork and suckling pig can be delicious grilled (perhaps over charcoal) or roasted. Look out for *aphelia*, a tender pork stew made with red wine and coriander

seeds, which does not often appear on hotel and restaurant menus.

Vegetable dishes and accompaniments include black-eyed beans *(louvia)*, potatoes, rice, green beans or peas, tomatoes, courgettes (zucchini) and aubergines. Fresh green salads are always available. 'Greek' or 'village-style' salads incorporate tomatoes and *feta* cheese. In hotels and at pool-sides you'll see mixed chef's salad, potato, egg and *Niçoise* salads.

## DESSERTS

Cheese offerings are limited to the local ewe's milk *halloumi* (salty and mild), Greek-style *feta* (a bit stronger) and some rather tired imports. Sometimes *graviera* is served – a local version of Swiss *gruyère* – as well as *kefalotyri* and *kaskavalli*.

*Charcoal-grilled meat (souvlakia) is the speciality at this Ayia Napa hotel.*

Concentrate instead on the fruit of Cyprus. Depending on the season, you'll be able to try the outstanding honeydew or cantaloupe melon, watermelon, cherries, peaches, figs, apricots, oranges, tangerines, plums, grapes, pomegranates, and more... You may also find wonderful yoghurt and honey, though not as often as in Greece.

Cypriot sweets are very sweet indeed. A speciality of Yeroskipos and Lefkara, *loukhoumi* is the sugar-dusted, jellied Turkish delight. Honey and nuts flavour *baklava*, a strudel-like pastry, and *kataifi*, a pastry which resembles Shredded Wheat. Another speciality of Cypriot pastry chefs, *loukoumades* are a kind of very sweet puffy doughnut dipped in syrup. The ice-cream, ices and sundaes can be excellent, and many hotels offer French-style pastries and tarts.

## DRINKS

In addition to a variety of soft drinks and mineral water, **105** there is excellent beer, brewed in Cyprus. Like the Greeks, Cypriots favour *ouzo*, the refreshing anis-flavoured apéritif. Pool-side drinks often include cooling Pimm's cup; and do try the heady, fruit brandy sours – which are to Cyprus what *piña colada* is to the Caribbean. Otherwise all the usual cocktails and drinks are available, but these are likely to be on the expensive side when they include imported spirits.

## WINES

Cyprus wines have been renowned since antiquity. Foremost among them is the sweet red Commandaria, originally produced for the Knights of St John at Kolossi. Celebrated as an apéritif or dessert wine, it is worth trying even if you usually eschew sweet wines. Sweet to dry wines of the sherry type are another Cypriot speciality.

Constantly improving in quality, Cypriot table wines equal the best similar vintages of Italy and Spain, and even some of the lesser wines of France. White wines are usually quite light but not sweet; the outstanding names include Keo Hock, White Lady, Aphrodite and Arsinoë. Bella Pais, a rather bubbly white, makes a good apéritif or dessert wine. Duc de Nicosie is the closest a Cyprus wine comes to being champagne. It is produced using the traditional French method for a quite honourable result.

Red wines are catching up to whites in quality and popularity – even in this warm climate. Keo Claret, Olympus Claret and Domaine d'Ahera in particular often have subtlety as well as body. Othello, a very well-known brand, can be outstanding (but not cheap) in vintage years – try the banner year of 1959. There are a few rosés; most people consider Coeur de Lion the best.

For an after-dinner drink, try some Cypriot brandy. In the more sophisticated category, Five Kings is one of the better-known brands. Filfar, a very strong liqueur, resembles Grand Marnier in taste.

# BLUEPRINT
## for a Perfect Trip

# AN A–Z SUMMARY OF PRACTICAL INFORMATION

> *Listed after some basic entries is the appropriate Greek expression, usually in the singular, plus some phrases that should help when you are seeking assistance. Accent marks are given to indicate stress.*

## A

### ACCOMMODATION ( ΞΕΝΟΔΟΧΕΙΟ; ΔΩΜΑΤΙΑ – xenodochío; *domátia)*

See CAMPING, YOUTH HOSTELS, HOTEL and RESTAURANT sections. In the high season (mid-June to October), try to book well in advance. The Cyprus Tourism Organization (see p. 132) produces a brochure listing various possibilities in each town. If you arrive without a booking, contact the CTO at the airport or in Nicosia, Larnaca, Limassol or Paphos for advice.

**Hotels.** Cyprus has hotels of all categories, from five-star luxury havens to one-star bed-and-breakfast pensions, as well as very pleasant apartment-hotels (classified A, B, C, and Tourist Apartments) and clean, simple guest houses. In general, standards are high and prices are reasonable compared with other resorts and islands. All hotels offer discounts during the low season, which for seaside resorts is from 1 November to 31 March and for hill resorts from 1 October to 30 June – excluding the Christmas/New Year and Easter holiday periods.

**Villas** may be rented through local agencies, or inquire at the CTO

| | |
|---|---|
| I'd like a single/double room | **Tha íthela éna monó/dipló domátio** |
| with bath/shower | **me bánio/dous** |
| What's the rate per night? | **Piá íne i timí giá mía níkta?** |

## AIRPORTS *(ΑΕΡΟΔΡΟΜΙΟ – aerodrómio)*

Larnaca International Airport, the principal air gateway to Cyprus, lies 6 km (3 miles) from Larnaca town and 50 km (30 miles) from Nicosia. Taxis are available into both cities, while shared taxis and mini-buses, scheduled frequently during the day, provide inexpensive transport for three or more passengers. A few local buses operate daily to Larnaca and Limassol.

A replacement for Nicosia airport – since 1974 on United Nations territory and no longer used for commercial flights – the Larnaca facility has been modernized and expanded to cope with increased air traffic into the Republic of Cyprus. Larnaca has a duty-free shop, snack bar, restaurant, currency exchange, car hire agencies, post office and tourist information office. At peak hours in the high season, check-in counters may be crowded and service somewhat slow, so arrive with plenty of time to spare (at least 1 hour) before flight departure.

Paphos International Airport, 11 km (7 miles) south-east of Paphos town on the west coast, handles freight and certain scheduled and charter services, easing the congestion at Larnaca. Paphos has a duty-free shop, currency-exchange facilities and restaurants.

The airport at Ercan in north Cyprus, served by flights from the mainland of Turkey only, has been declared by the Republic of Cyprus a prohibited port of entry and exit.

| | |
|---|---|
| Porter! Take these bags to the bus/taxi, please. | **Parakaló! Pigénete aftés tis aposkevés sto leoforío/taxi.** |

## ALPHABET *(see Language)*

## ANTIQUITIES *(antíkes)*

The purchase and export of antiquities is strictly regulated, and export permission must be granted by the Director of the Department of Antiquities, c/o Ministry of Communications and Works, Nicosia. It is illegal to remove antiquities, stones and other remains from any archaeological site, including the seabed.

## BICYCLE and MOTORCYCLE HIRE (ΕΝΟΙΚΙΑΣΕΙΣ ΠΟΔΗΛΑΤΩΝ – enikiásis podiláton; ΕΝΟΙΚΙΑΣΕΙΣ ΜΟΤΟ- ΣΥΚΛΕΤΤΩΝ – enikiásis motosiklettón)

You can hire bicycles and motorcycles from all towns. To operate a motorcycle, you must be at least 18 years of age and hold a driver's licence. It is obligatory to wear a crash helmet.

## CAMPING (ΚΑΤΑΣΚΗΝΩΣΗ– kataskínosi)

Official camp sites are licensed by the Cyprus Tourism Organiza- tion. Most provide electricity, toilets and showers, café-restaurant and food shop. The main sites are at Troodos; Polis 50 km (30 miles) north of Paphos; Forest Beach, east of Larnaca; Ayia Napa, near the village; and Governor's Beach near Limassol. The government per- mits a few other sites to operate on a provisional basis, especially those with basic facilities near restaurants.

Ask at the nearest CTO office (see p. 132). For local, unlisted camp sites, ask at the police station in the nearest town.

| | |
|---|---|
| Is there a campsite nearby? | **Ipárchi éna méros giá kataskínosi/'camping' edó kondá?** |
| We have a caravan (trailer). | **Échoume trochóspito.** |

## CAR HIRE (ΕΝΟΙΚΙΑΣΕΙΣ ΑΥΤΟΚΙΝΗΤΩΝ – enikiásis aftokiníton)

See also DRIVING. International and local car hire firms have offices in the major cities, and representatives at Larnaca and Paphos air- ports and at the main hotels. Rates are not cheap, but if you rent from a good local firm, you'll generally get good value. Some Cyprus firms charge slightly less than international agencies and provide equally good cars and service. Ask about reduced rates for weekly or monthly rentals. Note that the rate always includes un-limited mileage.

Reserve a car ahead of time – especially for the high season, when there often are not enough vehicles to go around. Air conditioning and automatic transmission are the exception rather than the rule; make any special requests in advance.

To hire a car, you must have a valid national licence (held for at least 2 years) or an International Driving Permit. Depending on the company, the minimum age is 21 to 25. A deposit is usually required unless you pay by credit card, accepted by the larger firms.

| | |
|---|---|
| I'd like to hire a car (tomorrow) | **Tha íthela na nikiáso éna aftokínito (ávrio)** |
| for one day/a week. | **giá mía iméra/mía evdomáda.** |
| Please include full insurance. | **Sas parakaló n simberilávete plíri asfália.** |

## CLIMATE

Cyprus boasts sunny skies and low humidity all the year round. On the coast, sea breezes temper the heat of July and August, though the thermometer has been known to hit 38°C (100°F) in Nicosia. Citizens of the capital beat a quick retreat to the coast or Troodos resorts during the hot days of summer. Days of sun (sea coast): 340.

January and February see snowfalls in the Troodos range – enough most years to allow some skiing. It rains occasionally between October and February, but there's plenty of sun, too, and the sea remains warm enough for some bathing.

Average daytime temperature in Nicosia:

| | J | F | M | A | M | J | J | A | S | O | N | D |
|---|---|---|---|---|---|---|---|---|---|---|---|---|
| Max °C | 15 | 16 | 19 | 24 | 29 | 34 | 37 | 37 | 33 | 28 | 22 | 17 |
| °F | 59 | 61 | 66 | 75 | 85 | 92 | 98 | 98 | 92 | 83 | 72 | 63 |
| Min °C | 5 | 5 | 7 | 10 | 14 | 18 | 21 | 21 | 18 | 14 | 10 | 7 |
| °F | 42 | 42 | 44 | 50 | 58 | 65 | 70 | 69 | 65 | 58 | 51 | 45 |

## CLOTHING

In summer, wear comfortable loose cotton clothing (synthetics are unsuitable in this climate). Nights can be cool, even in summer, so be sure to pack a sweater. In winter months (late November to March), you'll need a raincoat or light winter coat, a warm sweater or jacket, and perhaps a woollen outfit or two.

On the beach toplessness is generally tolerated; nudity in public is unacceptable. Take along a cover-up for the beach-bar – not just for modesty, but because cool breezes blow up.

Informality is the general rule, but in many hotels and restaurants people do dress up in the evening. So you may want to take something besides jeans and minimal sportswear: attractive dresses and skirts or trousers for women, jacket and tie for men. Women find knee-length skirts both cool and appropriate for visits to Orthodox churches and monasteries; men should wear long trousers and shirts.

## COMPLAINTS

Complaints don't often arise in this hospitable country, but should you have any problems, speak to the manager or proprietor of the establishment in question. Your complaints will usually receive prompt attention, since most Cypriots are anxious to please.

Among the sunniest and most friendly people in the world, Cypriots are also unfailingly polite – except occasionally behind the wheel of a car. If you have problems, they offer to help, give directions and call taxis for you.

## CRIME

There is still so little crime here that the few robberies make headlines. Unfortunately, this idyllic state of things may change fast, with the mass arrival of tourists and workers from nearby Mediterranean countries. So take the usual precautions of locking a car and depositing money and jewellery in the hotel safe.

## CUSTOMS AND ENTRY FORMALITIES

**Entry formalities and custom controls.** See also Driving. Most visitors need only a valid passport to enter Cyprus.

Legal points of entry are the ports of Larnaca, Limassol and Paphos and the international airports of Larnaca and Paphos. Visitors travelling via the airport of Ercan or the ports of Famagusta, Kyrenia or Karavostasi in the Turkish-controlled zone may not cross the border into the Republic of Cyprus.

The following chart shows what main duty-free items you may take into and out of Cyprus :

| Into: | Cigarettes | | Cigars | | Tobacco | Spirits | | Wine |
|---|---|---|---|---|---|---|---|---|
| Cyprus | 200 | or | 50 | or | 250 g | 1 L | and | 1 L |
| Australia | 200 | or | 250 | or | 250 g | 1 L | or | 1 L |
| Canada | 200 | and | 50 | and | 900 g | 1.1 L | or | 1.1 L |
| Eire | 200 | or | 50 | or | 250 g | 1 L | and | 2 L |
| New Zealand | 200 | or | 50 | or | 250 g | 1.1 L | and | 4.5 L |
| South Africa | 200 | and | 50 | and | 250 g | 1 L | and | 2 L |
| UK | 200 | or | 50 | or | 250 g | 1 L | and | 2 L |
| USA | 200 | and | 100 | and | * | 1 L | or | 1 L |

* a reasonable quantity

Customs formalities are usually minimal, although there are sometimes long waits for passport control. Your luggage may be opened for inspection.

**Currency restrictions.** Travellers may import local currency up to CY£50. There is no limit on the amount of foreign currency you may bring into Cyprus, but you must declare funds over $1,000. You may export foreign currency up to the amount imported and declared. No more than CY£50 may be taken out of the country.

I've nothing to declare.                    **Den écho típota na dilóso.**
It's for my personal use.                   **Íne giá prosopikí chrísi.**

# D

## DRIVING

**Entering Cyprus.** To bring your car into Cyprus you'll need:

- a valid driving licence or an International Driving Permit
- car registration papers
- a nationality plate or sticker.

It is compulsory to take out full third-party insurance coverage. Details are available at the port of entry or from the Registrar of Motor Vehicles:

1 Diogenis St., Engomi, Nicosia [tel. (02) 302600].

Cars may enter the country duty free for up to three months.

For further information, contact your local automobile association or the Cyprus Automobile Association:

12 Chr. Mylonas St., P.O. Box 2279, Nicosia 141 [tel. (02) 313233].

**Speed limits** are 50 kph in town, 100 kph on highways.

**Driving conditions.** British motorists will feel at home in Cyprus, where traffic keeps to the left. Everyone else should go slow at first, until the habit of driving on the left, overtaking (passing) on the right, becomes second nature. Use your horn if you need to, although it's prohibited in city centres 1–4 p.m. and after 9 p.m.

There are a few motorways (expressways) – notably the Nicosia–Limassol road, opened in 1984. Conditions on this super-highway are excellent, but beware of speeders. Otherwise, the larger roads are good to indifferent and the two-way thoroughfares often quite busy. Country roads may be mere cow paths, so you have to concentrate in case an animal or another car is coming from the opposite direction.

Although usually paved, 'main' mountain roads can be treacherous: one and a half lanes for two-way traffic is the rule; they are often pock-marked with potholes and generally have steep, hairpin turns. Only the fittest, most alert drivers should attempt these roads.

Cypriot drivers can be aggressive, know the roads and brook no interference – even though they, too, can have accidents. Narrow lanes and raised paved surfaces beside soft shoulders make it very hard to keep on course if a large vehicle coming the other way should force you to the edge on a two-lane route. City traffic is fairly orderly (there are traffic lights in all cities), and you'll encounter only minor traffic jams in Nicosia.

**Parking.** This can be a problem in central Nicosia, Limassol, Paphos and the old part of Larnaca. Fines may be handed out if you're in the way. Try to find a free or metered spot or a car park.

**Fuel and oil.** Prices compare favourably with those elsewhere in Europe. Diesel fuel is cheaper, and you can rent diesel cars. Petrol stations are plentiful around Nicosia, Limassol, Larnaca, Paphos and the coast, rather scarcer in the mountains. If you're setting out on an excursion, be sure the tank is full or nearly so, especially on Sundays or holidays, when many stations close. Petrol is sold by the litre. By and large, unleaded petrol is on sale only in the major towns – the international petrol stations provide a list of outlets.

**Road distances.** Distances in km between major tourist centres.

| | |
|---|---|
| Nicosia–Limassol | 80 |
| Nicosia–Larnaca | 51 |
| Limassol–Paphos | 72 |
| Limassol–Troodos | 51 |
| Paphos–Ayia Napa (coast road) | 184 |
| Larnaca–Limassol | 70 |

**Breakdowns.** Call your car hire agency, the Cyprus Automobile Association (tel. (02) 313233) or the police (tel. 119).

**Road signs.** Most are the standard pictographs used throughout Europe but you may encounter some written signs in English or Greek:

| | |
|---|---|
| ΑΔΙΕΞΟΔΟΣ | No through road |
| ΑΛΤ | Stop |

| | |
|---|---|
| ΑΝΩΜΑΛΙΑ ΟΔΟΣΤΡΩΜΑΤΟΣ | Bad road surface |
| ΑΠΑΓΟΡΕΥΕΤΑΙ Η ΑΝΑΜΟΝΗ | No waiting |
| ΑΠΑΓΟΡΕΥΕΤΑΙ Η ΕΙΣΟΔΟΣ | No entry |
| ΑΠΑΓΟΡΕΥΕΤΑΙ Η ΣΤΑΘΜΕΥΣΙΣ | No parking |
| ΔΙΑΒΑΣΙΣ ΠΕΖΩΝ | Pedestrian crossing |
| ΕΛΑΤΤΩΣΑΤΕ ΤΑΧΥΤΗΤΑΝ | Reduce speed |
| ΕΠΙΚΙΝΔΥΝΟΣ ΚΑΤΩΦΕΡΕΙΑ | Dangerous incline |
| ΟΔΙΚΑ ΕΡΓΑ | Roadworks in progress |
| ΚΙΝΔΥΝΟΣ | Caution |
| ΜΟΝΟΔΡΟΜΟΣ | One-way traffic |
| ΠΑΡΑΚΑΜΠΤΗΡΙΟΣ | Diversion (Detour) |
| ΠΟΔΗΛΑΤΑΙ | Cyclists |
| ΠΟΡΕΙΑ ΥΠΟΧΡΕΩΤΙΚΗ ΔΕΞΙΑ | Keep right |

| | |
|---|---|
| (International) Driving Permit | **(diethnís) ádia odigíseos** |
| Car registration papers | **ádia kikloforías** |
| Collision insurance | **asfália enandíon trítou** |
| Are we on the right road for ...? | **Ímaste sto sostó drómo giá ...?** |
| Full tank, please. | **Na to gemísete me venzíni.** |
| normal/super | **aplí/soúper, parakaló** |
| Check the oil/tyres/battery. | **Na eléchsete ta ládia/ta lásticha/ti bataría.** |
| I've had a breakdown. | **Épatha mía vlávi.** |
| There's been an accident. | **Égine éna distíchima.** |

# E

## ELECTRIC CURRENT

The standard current is 220/240 volts, 50 Hz AC; sockets are usually three-pin, as in the UK. Adaptors are available in hotels and shops. Most hotels and flats have 110-volt outlets for razors.

| | |
|---|---|
| I need an adaptor/battery, please. | **Chriázome éna metaschimatistí/ mia bataría, parakaló.** |

**EMBASSIES and CONSULATES** *(ΠΡΟΞΕΝΕΙΟ – proxenío;*
*ΠΡΕΣΒΕΙΑ – presvía)*

| | |
|---|---|
| **Australia** | Chancery, 4 Annis Comnenis Street, Nicosia; tel. (02) 473001. |
| **United Kingdom** | High Commission, Alexander Pallis Street, Nicosia; tel. (02) 473131. |
| **USA** | Embassy, Disotheon and Therissou Streets, Lycavitos, Nicosia; tel. (02) 465151. |

## EMERGENCIES

**Police, Fire Brigade, Ambulance** (island-wide)     199

| **Hospital** | Nicosia | (02) 45 11 11 |
|---|---|---|
| | Larnaca | (04) 63 03 12 |
| | Limassol | (05) 36 31 11 |
| | Paphos | (06) 23 23 64 |

These words are useful in difficult situations:

| Careful | **Prosochí** | Police | **Astinomía** |
|---|---|---|---|
| Help | **Voíthia** | Stop | **Stamatíste** |

## ETIQUETTE

Etiquette is informal, but it's customary to shake hands when greeting somebody or saying goodbye. Many Cypriots are so enthusiastic about visitors that they offer even complete strangers something to drink or eat, and you should try to accept. They love protracted conversations, and they'll try to induce you to chat for a while, even if you're in a hurry.

A few words of Greek from the visitor are appreciated but not really necessary; the polite phrases in English are just as welcome. Most people happily pose for photographs, and a copy sent to them makes a welcome thank you for a good holiday in their country.

**Meeting people.** It's impossible *not* to meet people. Conversations start casually anywhere – in shops, banks, tourist offices, hotels, museums, cafés – even simply asking directions. Cypriots are fascinated by foreigners. They also love to offer small presents – coffee, a drink, fruit, postcards. You should accept graciously.

Manners and mores among the young are fairly regulated. But in cities disco dancing and the cinema are a way of life. Young people can meet in discos or at the beach, and young Cypriots are friendly. Cypriot men do not 'pester' foreign women, and foreign men should be equally discreet with Cypriot women.

Cypriots show amazing warmth and friendliness, plus innate good manners. Visitors should do the same.

| | |
|---|---|
| How do you do? | **Ti kánete?** |
| How are you? | **Pos íste?** |
| Very well, thank you. | **Políkalá, efcharistó.** |

# GETTING TO CYPRUS

### By Air: Scheduled Flights
Direct daily flights link London to Larnaca, with less frequent service from Manchester and Birmingham.

Connecting services operate to Larnaca from major cities in North America, including New York, Miami, Los Angeles and San Francisco.

Most Australian travellers to Cyprus fly by way of Athens, while the most direct route from New Zealand is via Sydney and Athens.

The usual routing to Larnaca from South Africa involves changing planes in Lusaka or Athens.

### By Air: Charter Flights and Package Tours
British tour operators offer a wide variety of packages from London. The price includes air travel (on a group fare basis), transfers and either hotel or apartment accommodation, the former with or without meals. Car hire at discounted rates is optional.

### By Boat
Car and passenger ferries run at regular intervals between Piraeus and Limassol, a journey of three days.

## GUIDES, INTERPRETERS (xenagós; dierminéas) and TOURS

**Guide-interpreters.** Professional authorized guide-interpreters speaking English and other languages can be engaged through hotels and specialized agencies.

| | |
|---|---|
| We'd like an English-speaking guide. | **Tha thélame éna xenagó pou na milá angliká.** |
| I need an English interpreter. | **Chriázome éna ánglo dierminéa.** |

**Boat trips.** Ask at the tourist office about boat excursions and short cruises in Cypriot waters. The only legal seaports of entry at present are Limassol, Larnaca and Paphos. The main port of entry is Limassol, served by several ferry lines and cruise companies.

| | |
|---|---|
| Where's the nearest bus stop? | **Pou íne o kondinóteros stathmós ton leoforíon?** |
| When's the next boat/bus to ...? | **Póte févgi to epómeno plío/leoforío giá ...?** |
| I want a ticket to ... | **Thélo éna isitírio giá ...** |
| single (one-way) | **apló** |
| return (round-trip) | **me epistrofí** |
| first/second class | **próti/deftéra thési** |
| Will you tell me when to get off? | **Tha mou píte pou na katevó?** |

## LANGUAGE

**The alphabet.** Signs in towns and cities usually appear in Greek and English. But in the villages, a familiarity with Greek can be useful.

The Greek alphabet does not need to be a mystery to you. The table below lists the Greek letters in their capital and small forms, followed by the letter they correspond to in English.

| | | | | | |
|---|---|---|---|---|---|
| **A** α a | as in bar | | **H** η i | like **ee** in meet |
| **B** β v | | | **Θ** θ th | as in thin |
| **Γ** γ g | as in go* | | **I** ι i | like **ee** in meet |
| **Δ** δ d | like th in this | | **K** κ k | |
| **E** ε e | as in get | | **Λ** λ l | |
| **Z** ζ z | | | **M** μ m | |
| **N** ν n | | | **Y** υ i | like **ee** in meet |
| **Ξ** ξ x | like **ks** as in thanks | | **T** τ t | |
| **O** ο o | as in got | | **X** χ ch | as in Scottish lo**ch** |
| **Π** π p | | | **Ψ** ψ ps | as in ti**ps**y |
| **P** ρ r | | | **Ω** ω o | as in bone |
| **Σ** σ, ς s | as in kiss | | **OY** ου | as in soup |
| **Φ** φ f | | | | |

\* except before **i**- and **e**-sounds, when it's pronounced like **y** in yes

Greek Cypriots converse in a dialect that dates back to the time of Homer. With a distinctive vocabulary and pronunciation (the 'ch' sound is strong), it is all but unintelligible to a Greek from the mainland. The written language, however, conforms to that of Greece.

In the country or the mountains, communication may be a problem, but invariably sign language saves the day. And everybody seems to know someone (a young student, perhaps) within shouting distance who can translate.

If you want to try Greek, consult the Berlitz phrase book GREEK FOR TRAVELLERS. It covers practically all the situations you're likely to encounter during your Cyprus travels.

Following are a few phrases you'll want to use often:

| | |
|---|---|
| Good morning | **Kaliméra** |
| Please | **Parakaló** |
| Good afternoon | **Kalispéra** |
| Thank you | **Efcharistó** |
| Good night | **Kaliníkta** |
| Goodbye | **Chérete** |
| Do you speak English? | **Miláte angliká?** |
| I don't speak Greek. | **Den miló ellinniká.** |

## LAUNDRY and DRY CLEANING (ΠΛΥΝΤΗΡΙΟ – *plintírio*; ΣΤΕΓΝΟΚΑΘΑΡΙΣΤΗΡΙΟ – *stegnokatharistírio*)

Much of the year you can easily do your own small-article laundry; in the warm climate, clothes dry quickly. Some hotels offer one-day express service for an extra charge. Pressing can usually be done by afternoon if you give it in before 9 a.m. Otherwise count 2–3 days for laundry and dry cleaning. Some towns have launderette facilities and quick dry-cleaning services.

| | |
|---|---|
| Where's the nearest laundry/dry-cleaners? | **Pou íne to kondinótero plintírio/stegnokatharistírio?** |
| When will it be ready? | **Póte tha íne étimo?** |
| I must have this for tomorrow morning. | **Prépi na íne étimo ávrio to proí.** |

## LOST PROPERTY

Cypriots are known for their honesty, and lost money and jewellery are often recovered by the owners. If you lose something, it will probably be kept for you where you left it. Otherwise, ask at the nearest police station.

Lost children will invariably be taken care of. If you lose your child, tell people around you, then the police.

| | |
|---|---|
| I've lost my wallet/handbag/passport. | **Échasa to portofóli mou/ti tsánda mou/to diavatirió mou.** |

## MAPS

The Cyprus Tourism Organization gives comprehensive island maps and town plans of Nicosia, Limassol, Larnaca, Paphos and the Troodos region. Various companies publish excellent maps of Cyprus, indicating sights and sites, even hotel facilities available.

The maps in this book were prepared by Falk-Verlag, Hamburg. **121**

| I'd like a street plan of ... | **Tha íthela éna odikó chárti** |
| | **tis ...** |
| a road map of this region | **éna chárti aftís tis periochís** |

## MEDICAL MATTERS

To be completely at ease, take out health insurance to cover any risk of illness and accident while on holiday. Your travel agent or insurance company will be able to advise you. (The Cyprus social services offer no free treatment to foreign visitors.) There are capable doctors and dentists in cities and larger towns, as well as adequate hospital facilities (see also EMERGENCIES). All doctors are educated abroad and speak a second language, usually English.

Stomach upsets should not be a problem, as hotels and restaurants usually observe high standards of cleanliness. Tap-water is safe to drink.

The sun can bronze you, but also burn you to a crisp. Take it in very easy doses at first (not more than 15 minutes a day in spring and summer), and use a sun-screen, particularly if you have delicate skin.

**Pharmacies** (ΦΑΡΜΑΚΕΙΟ – *farmakío*) are recognized by the sign outside - a red cross on a white background (for opening hours see p. 124). Certain chemists offer 24-hour service – check lists in local newspapers or ring a special information number (02) 462618. Most medicines sold in the UK, USA and Canada or in Europe are available, but often require a prescription. Pharmacists can generally advise on minor problems such as cuts, sunburn, blisters, throat infections and gastric disorders.

| Where's the nearest (all-night) pharmacy? | **Pou íne to kondinótero (dianikterévon) farmakio?** |
| I need a doctor/dentist. | **Chriázome éna giatró/odontogiatró.** |
| an ambulance | **éna asthenofóro** |
| hospital | **nosokomío** |
| I have ... | **Écho ...** |
| **122** sunburn | **éngavma apó ton ílio** |

| a headache | **ponokéfalo** |
| a fever | **piretós** |
| an upset stomach | **pónossti kiliá** |

## MONEY MATTERS (see also OPENING HOURS)

**Currency.** The Cyprus pound (CY£) is divided into 100 cents.
Coins: 1, 2, 5, 10 and 20 cents.
Banknotes: 50 cents and CY£1, 5 and 10.
For currency restrictions, see CUSTOMS AND ENTRY FORMALITIES.

**Currency exchange.** Hotels change money and travellers' cheques,
but banks (ΤΡΑΠΕΖΑ – *trápeza*) give much better rates – although
the formalities can take a few minutes to half an hour.

**Eurocheques, travellers' cheques, credit cards** ('eurocheque',
'travellers' cheque', *pistotikí kárta*). Eurocheques are in widespread
use in Cyprus. Travellers' cheques, widely accepted, are best cashed
at a bank. Major credit cards are welcome as payment in most city
shops, hotels, and restaurants, as well as by all the international and
better local car hire firms. Don't forget your passport.

**Cash.** US dollars and other strong currencies may be accepted by
shops or restaurants – but you'll probably get a poor exchange rate.

| I want to change some pounds/ dollars. | **Thélo n alláxo merikés líres/ meriká dollária.** |
| Do you accept travellers' cheques? | **Pérnete 'travellers' cheques'?** |
| Can I pay with this credit card? | **Boró na pliróso me aftí ti pistotikí kárta?** |

N

## NEWSPAPERS and MAGAZINES *(efimerída; periodikó)*
There is a good selection of European periodicals and the major
American weekly news magazines in larger towns. Foreign news-
papers arrive 1–2 days after publication, depending on where you

are. The *Cyprus Mail*, an English-language daily, has current news coverage. The *Cyprus Weekly* (in English) carries lively features and helpful information. *Cyprus Time Out* is the publication to consult for listings of leisure events.

Have you any English-language newspapers? **Échete anglikés efimerídes?**

## OPENING HOURS

**Archaeological sites.** The major sites remain open year-round from 7.30 a.m. until dusk, including Sundays and holidays, except Orthodox Easter Sunday.

**Banks.** In general, hours are 8.15 a.m.–12.30 p.m. Monday to Friday. Some banks in tourist centres open for currency exchange only from 4–6 p.m.

**Museums.** Opening hours are subject to constant change. Check times with the local Cyprus Tourism Organization when you first arrive. As a general rule, most museums open 7.30 or 8 a.m. on the coast, 8.30 or 9 a.m. in Nicosia. Most, but not all, now stay open during the lunch hour. Most, but not all, close Saturday afternoons and Sundays.

**Pharmacies.** Except for the chemists on 24-hour duty, shops open 7.30 or 8 a.m.–1 p.m. and 3 or 4–7 p.m., Monday to Friday (morning only on Wednesday and Saturday).

**Post offices.** Generally open 8 a.m.–1.30 p.m. from Monday to Friday. The main post office in Nicosia is open later in summer.

**Restaurants.** Lunch is normally served 1–3.30 p.m. and dinner 9–10.30 p.m., but many restaurants continue to serve till midnight.

**Shops.** Nearly all establishments open 8 a.m.–1 p.m. and 4–7 p.m. summer weekdays (mornings only, Wednesday and Saturday). From October to April, most afternoon hours are 2.30–5.30 p.m. In summer, the siesta is sacred: everything grinds to a halt from about 2 p.m. for at least two hours. You'd be wise, too, simply to relax at the beach, at the poolside or in your hotel room.

## PHOTOGRAPHY

Leading brands of film are usually available in Cyprus.

For security reasons, it is not allowed to photograph military installations – especially along the border of the Turkish-controlled zone.

Be sure to ask permission before using your camera in a museum.

| | |
|---|---|
| I'd like some film for this camera. | **Tha íthela éna film giaftí tí michaní.** |
| black-and-white film colour prints | **asprómavro film énchromo film** |
| colour slides | **énchromo film giá thiafánies** |
| 35-mm film | **éna film triánda pénde milimétr** |
| super-8 | **soúper-októ** |
| How long will it take? | **Póte tha íne étimo?** |
| May I take a picture? | **Boró na páro mía fotografía?** |

## PLANNING YOUR BUDGET

Here are some average prices in Cypriot pounds (CY£). However, all prices must be regarded as approximate.

**Airport transfer.** Taxi to Larnaca town CY£1.50, to Nicosia CY£11, shared taxi to Nicosia CY£1.35, to Limassol CY£1.60, Paphos (from Larnaca) CY£3.20.

**Bicycle and motorcycle hire.** Bicycles CY£1.50–2.50 per day, motorcycles CY£3–15 per day.

**Buses.** Larnaca town–Nicosia CY£0.70, Larnaca town–Limassol CY£0.90, Larnaca town to Paphos (via Limassol) CY£1.90, Limassol–Pano Platres CY£1.

**Camping.** From CY£1.50 per day for tent or caravan plus CY£0.25 per person per day for services and taxes. Caravans (trailers) can be rented from CY£8–10 per day, plus delivery charges.

**Car hire.** Rates per day for 1–6 days in summer season (unlimited mileage); Austin Mini CY£16, Ford Escort CY£17, Opel Kadett CY£18.50, Subaru CY£20, Mini-bus CY£25.

**Cigarettes.** Foreign brands manufactured under licence in Cyprus CY£0.45–0.70, imported CY£1.20 per packet.

**Entertainment.** Cinema CY£1.25–2.00; discotheque (admission and one drink) CY£3–5; cabaret (admission, first drink, show and dancing) CY£3.

**Guides.** CY£21.85 per half-day, CY£34.38 per day, 50% more on Sundays, 100% on public holidays, CY£2.33 overtime per hour.

**Hairdressers.** Man's haircut (with wash) CY£3.50. Woman's shampoo and set or blow-dry CY£4, permanent wave CY£10–12.

**Hotels.** Double room with bath: 5-star CY£60–100, 4-star CY£35–67, 3-star CY£26–40, 2-star CY£15–36, 1-star CY£12–14.

**Meals and drinks**. Continental breakfast CY£1.50–3.50, lunch or dinner in fairly good establishment CY£4–7, coffee and soft drinks CY£0.40–0.75, glass of wine or beer CY£0.50–1, brandy sour CY£0.80–1.25, gin and tonic CY£1.25–1.75.

**Sports.** Use of hotel beach facilities and/or tennis courts CY£1–3 per half-hour; water-skiing CY£8–10 per half hour, windsurfing CY£3 per hour, sailing CY£4–6 per hour, motor boats CY £8 per hour or CY£30 per day.

**Taxis.** Initial charge CY£0.55, plus about CY£0.21 per km in towns. Minimum charge CY£0.75.

## POLICE (ΑΣΤΥΝΟΜΙΑ – astinomía)

You probably won't see many policemen, but they are around and they invariably prove friendly and helpful. You'll recognize the traffic police by their white gloves and sleeves. The Port Police sport blue uniforms. Regular police also wear blue and cruise around in dark blue and white police cars. They usually speak some English.

Island-wide, the police emergency number is 199.

| | |
|---|---|
| Where's the nearest police station? | **Pou íne to kondinótero astinomikó tmíma?** |

## POST OFFICES (ΤΑΧΥΔΡΟΜΕΙΟ – tachidromío)

Post offices deal only with mail, not telecommunications. In Nicosia, the central post office is situated in Eleftheria Square.

If you don't know in advance where you'll be staying, have your mail sent *poste restante* (general delivery).

| | |
|---|---|
| Where's the (nearest) post office/ telephone office? | **Pou íne to kodinótero tachidromío/CYTA?** |
| Have you received any mail for ...? | **Échete grámmata giá ...?** |
| A stamp for this letter/ postcard, please. | **Éna grammatósimo giaftó to grámma/graftí tin kárta, parakaló.** |
| express (special delivery) | **exprés** |
| airmail | **aeroporikós** |
| registered | **sistiméno** |

## PUBLIC HOLIDAYS (argíes)

In addition to their own national holidays, Cypriots also celebrate certain Greek holidays. Offices close on the following days. Shops remain open on certain holidays: ask locally as to which ones.

| | | |
|---|---|---|
| 1 January | *Protochroniá* | New Year's Day |
| 6 January | *ton Theofanío* | Epiphany |
| 25 March | *Ikostí Pémti Martíou (tou Evangelismoú)* | Greek Independence Day |
| 1 April | *Iméra enárxeos kipriakoú agónos giá tin anexartisía* | Cyprus Struggle Day* |

| 1 May | *Protomagiá* | Labour Day |
| 3 August | *epétios tou thanátou tou Archiepiskópou Makaríou tou trítou* | Anniversary of the death of Archbishop Makarios III |
| 15 August | *Dekapendágoustos (tis Panagías)* | Assumption Day |
| 1 October | *Iméra tis anexartisías tis Kíprou* | Cyprus Independence Day |
| 28 October | *Ikostí Ogdói Oktovríou 'Ochi'* | ('No') Day, commemorating Greek defiance of Italian ultimatum and invasion of 1940. |
| 25 December | *Christoúgenna* | Christmas Day |
| 26 December | *epávrios ton Christoúgenna* | Boxing Day |
| Movable dates: | *Katharí Deftéra* | 1st Day of Lent: Ash Monday |
| | *Megáli Paraskeví* | Good Friday |
| | *Deftéra tou Pás̃cha* | Easter Monday |

*Note:* The dates on which the movable holidays are celebrated often differ from those in other European countries.

Are you open tomorrow?     **'Iste aniktí ávrio?**

\* Granted from year to year by decision of the Council of Ministers.

## PUBLIC TRANSPORT

Cyprus has no railway system and the bus service is not always frequent or reliable. Private and shared taxis fill the transport gap.

# R

## RADIO and TELEVISION *(radio; tileórasi)*

CyBC (Cyprus Broadcasting Corporation) carries programmes and news in English, plus a good selection of music, throughout the day. The BBC World Service transmits daily 6 a.m.–2.15 a.m. The BFBS (British Forces Broadcasting Service) offers daily local and UK news bulletins and commentary, as well as music.

The Republic of Cyprus has only one television network. Foreign films and serials (usually in English, sometimes in other languages) are shown nightly beginning around 9 or 10 p.m. Short newscasts in Greek, Turkish and English are given 6–6.30 p.m.

## SMOKING: Cigarettes, cigars and tobacco *(tsigára; poúra; kapnós)*

Smokers usually find what they need in general stores selling gifts, magazines and sundries. International brands produced under licence in Cyprus can be purchased at very low prices; imported tobacco products cost approximately twice as much.

| | |
|---|---|
| A packet of .../A box of matches, please. | **Éna pakéto .../Éna koutí spírta, parakaló.** |
| filter-tipped/without filter | **me fíltro/chorís fíltro** |

## TAXIS *(ΤΑΞΙ - taxí)*

Vehicles are metered and rates are low, making private taxis a favourite form of transport. Many visitors, daunted by the difficult road conditions, travel around the island exclusively by taxi.

**Shared taxis and mini-buses** (ΕΠΙΒΑΤΙΚΑ ΤΑΞΙ - *epivatikó taxí;* ΜΙΚΡΑ ΠΟΥΛΜΑΝ -*mikrá poúlman*) run according to a schedule, carrying several passengers for a very reasonable fixed price. This is a great way to get around the island. You can hail a taxi on the street or call for one by telephone. The numbers of the various private companies are listed in the telephone directory under 'Taxi'.

| | |
|---|---|
| Where can I get a taxi/ shared taxi/mini-bus? | **Pou boró na vro éna taxí/ epivatikó taxí/mikrá poúlman?** |
| May I have a place | **Thélo mía thési** |

**129**

| | |
|---|---|
| in this taxi for ...? | **se taxí giá ...?** |
| What's the fare to ...? | **Piá íne i timí giá ...?** |

## TELEPHONES: and telegrams *(tiléfono; tilegráfima)*

Telephone, telex and telegram communications come under the auspices of the Cyprus Telecommunications Authority (CYTA). Automatic service operates for local, long-distance and international calls. The direct-dialling codes to main Cypriot cities are:

| | | | |
|---|---|---|---|
| Nicosia | 02 | Limassol | 05 |
| Ayia Napa | 03 | Paphos | 06 |
| Larnaca | 04 | | |

The code for Cyprus from outside the country is 357.

### Telephone Spelling Code

| | | | |
|---|---|---|---|
| A | Aléxandros | N | Nikólaos |
| B | Vasílios | Ξ | Xenofón |
| Γ | Geórgios | O | Odisséfs |
| Δ | Dimítrios | Π | Periklís |
| E | Eléni | P | Ródos |
| Z | Zoï | Σ | Sotírios |
| H | Iraklís | T | Timoléon |
| Θ | Theódoros | Y | Ipsilántis |
| I | Ioánnis | Φ | Fótios |
| K | Konstantínos | X | Chrístos |
| Λ | Leonídas | Ψ | Psáltis |
| M | Menélaos | Ω | Oméga |

In most hotels you can dial long distance from your room, but a surcharge may be added to the bill. Standard rates and other information are available from the long-distance operator (194).

For local calls, most cafés, newspaper kiosks and food shops will allow you to use their phones.

| | |
|---|---|
| I want to send a telegram to ... | **Thélo na stílo éna tilegráfima sto ...** |
| Can you get me this number in ...? | **Boríte na mou párete aftó ton arithmó ...?** |

| reverse-charge (collect) call | **plirotéo apó to paralípti** |
|---|---|
| person-to-person (personal) call | **prosopikí klísi** |

## TIME DIFFERENCES

The chart below shows the time difference between Cyprus and various cities in winter (GMT + 2). In summer Cypriot clocks are put forward 1 hour.

| New York | London | **Cyprus** | Jo'burg | Sydney | Auckland |
|---|---|---|---|---|---|
| 5 a.m. | 10 a.m. | **noon** | noon | 9 p.m. | 11 p.m. |

What time is it?                **Ti óra íne?**

## TIPPING

Service charges are included in hotel, restaurant and taverna bills. But 'a little extra' is always appreciated, especially for good service.

Average tips:

| | |
|---|---|
| Hotel porter, per bag | CY£0.50–1 |
| Maid, per day | CY£0.50–1 |
| Waiter/barman | 5–10% (optional) |
| Taxi driver | 10% (optional) |
| Tour guide (private) | around 10% |
| Tour guide (group tour) | from CY£0.50–1 per day |
| Hairdresser | 10–15% |

## TOILETS (ΑΠΟΧΩΡΗΤΗΡΙΑ - *apohoritíria*)

Public conveniences exist in larger towns, but not in any great numbers. Museums often have clean facilities, and the ones on the government-run 'tourist beaches' are excellent. Toilets are generally signed in English and Greek, with silhouettes of men and women. If you use the facilities in cafés, restaurants and hotels, it is customary to buy at least a coffee in exchange.

Where are the toilets?                **Pou íne ta apohoritíra?**

131

**TOURIST INFORMATION OFFICES** *(grafío pliroforión tourismoú)*

The Cyprus Tourism Organization, or CTO (*Kypriakós Organismós Tourismoú - KOT*) is a gold-mine of information, and its staff readily field all your questions, and have brochures and maps to help you plan your trip.

**UK**       213 Regent Street, London, W1R 8DA; tel. (071) 734 9822, fax 287 6534.

**USA**      13 E 40th Street, New York, NY 10016; tel. (212) 683 5280, fax 683 5282.

In Cyprus the CTO maintains offices at Larnaca airport, open day and night (tel. [04] 65 43 89) and in the major tourist centres:

**Nicosia**    35 Aristokyprou Street, Laiki Yitonia; tel. (02) 444264.
**Limassol**   15 Spyrou Araouzou Street; tel. (05) 36 27 56.
**Larnaca**    Democratias Square at Zenon Street; tel. (04) 65 43 22.
**Paphos**     3 Gladstone Street; tel. (06) 23 28 41. Airport; tel. (06) 23 68 33.
**Ayia Napa**  17 Arch. Makarios Ave; tel. (03) 72 17 96.

Where's the tourist office?     **Pou íne to grafío tourismoú?**

**WATER** *(neró)*

Tap water is safe to drink and is delicious in the Troodos mountains, where it comes fresh from the springs. Still and fizzy mineral waters are bottled on Cyprus; imported waters are available too.

a bottle of mineral water        **éna boukáli metallikó neró**
fizzy (carbonated)/still         **me/chorís anthrakikó**

**WEIGHTS and MEASURES**

The ancient units of weights and measures have been replaced by the precision of the international metric system. Grams and kilograms have elbowed aside the traditional drams and okes. On the roads, kilometres are erasing the miles. And litres have superseded gallons – with one sturdy exception: beer is still drunk by the pint. (For the historical record, 400 drams = 1 oke = 2.8 pounds.)

## Fluid measures

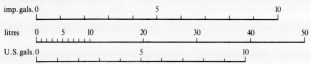

## Weight

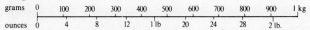

## Distance

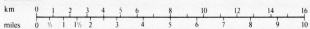

**YOUTH HOSTELS** *(ΞΕΝΩΝΑΣ ΝΕΩΝ – xenónas néon)*
Only members of the International Youth Hostels Association may stay at Cyprus's youth hostels:

**Nicosia** 13 Prince Charles Street (opposite Asty Hotel); tel. (02) 444808.
**Paphos** E. Venizelos Avenue; tel. (06) 232588.
**Troodos** Former Olympos Hotel (summer only); tel. (05) 415429.
**Limassol** 120 Ankara Street (behind Limassol Castle); tel. (05) 363749.
**Larnaca** Nicolaou Rossou Street (near St Lazarus Church).
For further information contact the Cyprus Youth Hostels Association, PO Box 1328, Nicosia, Cyprus.

## SOME USEFUL EXPRESSIONS

| | |
|---|---|
| yes/no | ne/óchi |
| please/thank you | parakaló/efcharistó |
| excuse me/you're welcome | me sinchoríte/parakaló |
| where/when/how | pou/póte/pos |
| how long/how far | póso keró/póso makriá |
| yesterday/today/tomorrow | chthes/símera/ávrio |
| day/week/month/year | iméra/evdomáda/mínas/chrónos |
| left/right | aristerá/dexiá |
| up/down | epáno/káto |
| good/bad | kalós/kakós |
| big/small | megálos/mikrós |
| cheap/expensive | ftinós/akrivós |
| open/closed | aniktós/klistós |
| here/there | edó/ekí |
| free (vacant)/occupied | eléftheri/kratiméni |
| early/late | norís/argá |
| easy/difficult | éfkolos/dískolos |
| Does anybody here speak English? | Milá kanís angliká? |
| What does this mean? | Ti siméni aftó? |
| I don't understand. | Den katalavéno. |
| Please write it down. | Parakaló grápste to. |
| Is there an admission charge? | Prépi na pliróso ísodo? |
| Waiter, please! | Garsóni (garçon), parakaló! |
| I'd like ... | Tha íthela ... |
| How much is that? | Póso káni aftó? |
| Have you something less expensive? | Échete káti ftinótero? |
| What time is it? | Ti óra íne? |
| Just a minute. | Éna leptó. |
| Help me, please. | Voithíste me, parakaló. |

# Index

References to main entries are in bold, those to photographs are in italic.

**136**